MISFITS IN INDUSTRY

MISFITS IN INDUSTRY

Edited by

Pasquale A. Carone, M.D.
South Oaks Hospital
Amityville, New York

Sherman N. Kieffer, M.D.
State University of New York
at Stony Brook

Leonard W. Krinsky, Ph.D.
South Oaks Hospital
Amityville, New York

and

Stanley F. Yolles, M.D.
State University of New York
at Stony Brook

SP MEDICAL & SCIENTIFIC BOOKS
a division of Spectrum Publications, Inc.
New York • London

Distributed by Halsted Press
A Division of John Wiley & Sons

New York   Toronto   London   Sydney

Copyright © 1978 Spectrum Publications, Inc.

SPECTRUM PUBLICATIONS, INC.
175-20 Wexford Terrace, Jamaica, N.Y. 11432

Library of Congress Cataloging in Publication Data

Main entry under title:

Misfits in industry.

    Based on proceedings of a conference held at Stony
Brook, N.Y., in March, 1977.
    Includes index.
    1. Personnel management–Congresses. 2. Psychology,
Industrial--Congresses. 3. Industrial psychiatry–
HF5549.M527   158.7   78-7386
ISBN 0-89335-045-1

Distributed solely by the Halsted Press Division of John Wiley & Sons, Inc.
New York, New York
ISBN 0-470-26447-0

In memory of Joseph Lionello, M.D.

1898 - 1978

A dedicated physician, a colleague

and warm friend

Contributors

Joseph S. Barbaro, C.S.W.
Executive Director
Catholic Charities
Diocese of Rockville Centre

The Honorable Herbert Bienstock
Regional Commissioner of Labor Statistics
U.S. Department of Labor

Penny W. Budoff, M.D.
Assistant Professor
Department of Family Medicine
School of Medicine
Health Sciences Center
State University of New York at Stony
  Brook

Patrick F. Carone, M.D.
Assistant Professor
Department of Psychiatry
Yale School of Medicine

Luther A. Cloud, M.D.
Assistant Vice President &
  Associate Medical Director
Equitable Life Assurance Society of
  America

Thomas Conley
Personnel Relations Representative
Grumman Aerospace Corporation

Anthony J. Costaldo
AFL-CIO Representative
United Way of Nassau-Suffolk

Nan Dietrich
Jesuit Program for Living and Learning

Daniel Friedman, M.D.
Associate Professor
Department of Family Medicine
School of Medicine
Health Sciences Center
State University of New York at Stony
  Brook

Maurice Goldenhar, M.D.
Director of Family Practice
South Nassau Communities Hospital
            and
Assistant Professor
Department of Family Medicine
School of Medicine
Health Sciences Center
State University of New York at Stony
  Brook

Norman Goodman, Ph.D.
Chairman
Department of Sociology
State University of New York at Stony
  Brook

CONTRIBUTORS

Arthur D. Haggerty, Ph.D.
Director
Graduate Program in Health Care Adminis-
   tration
C.W. Post Center
Long Island University

Calvin L. Hutchings, M.A.
Counselling Psychologist
Air Line Pilots Association

Stuart L. Keill, M.D.
Chairman
Department of Psychiatry and Psychology
Nassau County Medical Center

Sherman N. Kieffer, M.D.
Professor and Vice Chairman
Department of Psychiatry and
   Behavioral Science
School of Medicine
Health Sciences Center
State University of New York at Stony
   Brook

Carroll G. Kitts
Manager
Employee Benefits
AIL, A Division of Cutler-Hammer

Dianne Knight, C.S.W.
Director of Social Services
South Oaks Hospital

Daniel E. Knowles
Director of Personnel
Grumman Aerospace Corporation

Gottfried F. Lehmann, M.D.
Medical Director
The Long Island Rail Road

Sanford V. Lenz
Labor Education Specialist
New York State School of Industrial and
   Labor Relations
Cornell University

Duncan R. MacMaster, M.D.
Private Practice
   and
Consultant, Connecticut Department of
   Vocational Rehabilitation

Edward H. Malone, M.D.
Clinical Director
South Oaks Hospital

Robert L. Meineker, M.D.
Director of Psychiatric Ambulatory
   Services
St. Vincent's Hospital
   and
Psychiatric Consultant to the Continental
   Insurance Company

Vicki Moss
Counselor
"Women Working"—Federally-funded
   Project for Unemployed and Under-
   employed Women
Bergen County, New Jersey

Walter S. Neff, Ph.D.
Professor Emeritus
New York University
   and
Professor of Psychiatry (Psychology)
School of Medicine
Health Sciences Center
State University of New York at Stony
   Brook

Ed Nelson
Senior Counselor
Local 504
Transport Workers Union

Tadao Ogura, M.D.
Staff Psychiatrist
South Oaks Hospital

Philippe F. Scholten
Director of Placement and Employee
  Relations
European American Bank

William Sims, M.A.
Placement Coordinator
The Rehabilitation Institute

Tracy Smith
Deputy Inspector
Nassau County Police Department

Frederick E. Snyder, M. Phil, Ph.D., J.D.
Graduate Fellow
Harvard Law School

Introduction

The purpose of the conference and the preparation of this volume was to bring together members of various disciplines who would evaluate the problems of the under-trained, over-trained and mistrained, and hopefully offer certain solutions.

"Misfits In Industry" is the result of the seventh annual conference on the problems of industrial psychiatric medicine which has been sponsored by South Oaks Foundation and the Department of Psychiatry and Behavioral Science at the Health Sciences Center, State University of New York at Stony Brook. It has always been our contention that the industrial workers of our country comprise a unique group with specific problems. In the past we have investigated the problems of drug abuse in industry, alcoholism in industry, the emotionally troubled employee, and the specific problems which women in industry must face.

The young people of our country have had to suddenly adapt to changes in the socioeconomic climate which must be seen as revolutionary rather than evolutionary. In a period of perhaps less than a decade we have moved from full employment to an extremely tight job market. It was but a short time ago that each young person was told that the attainment of a college degree was virtually a passport to success and that each person could choose the field in which he wished to dedicate himself. Suddenly our young people have found that they have apparently been deceived. They have gone ahead and pursued higher education, have trained themselves for fields such as teachers, computer technicians, etc., only to find that there are no jobs available.

For the first time since the Great Depression, our nation is confronted with a large disaffected population. We have people who are over-trained for what they are offered, undertrained for some of the jobs available and mistrained for the employment world in which we live.

Our purpose with the conference and book was to bring together representatives of management, labor, the academic world, the mental health disciplines, medicine and government. Each of these disciplines is integrally involved with the welfare of our citizenry. Each approaches problems in a different way but all share the goal of how to most effectively deal with those people who have come to be known as "Misfits In Industry."

There are important findings in this book. We learned for example, that the problem of misfits may be of short duration. A representative from government indicates that there may well be a shortage of trained people within the next decade. Most of the other participants, however, do not see such a rosy future and what is being found is that physical illnesses, and psychiatric and psychological disorders are some of the by-products of the troubled world in which the "Misfit In Industry" must try to find a place. Healthy controversy is seen particularly in the apparent attack on the school guidance counselors by our representative from management. It is his belief that counselors in education plants are giving false signals, incorrect data, and are advising students to pursue studies in areas where there are simply no jobs.

This volume, and the meeting upon which it was based, attracted a large number of prominent and knowledgeable people in their various fields, and offers certain solutions. As we expected, many more questions were raised than were answered. Perhaps this is the healthiest way to approach the problem, for it opens up areas of controversy and questions which must be answered by all of us.

Acknowledgments

This book is the product of the seventh annual conference sponsored by The South Oaks Foundation, Inc. and the Medical School of the State University of New York at Stony Brook, held on March 24th and 25th, 1977. In the spring of each year, problems in industrial psychiatric medicine are our principal focus of interest.

We are grateful to our Board of Directors for actively supporting this conference.

The conference could not have been held, and the volume not completed without the active involvement of all of our speakers and panelists. They were most cooperative in providing us with copies of their remarks and actively participating in the editorial process.

The real spadework fell to two of our South Oaks staff members who made it possible for us to proceed smoothly and efficiently. We especially commend Lynn S. Black, Director of Community Relations, and Catherine T. Martens, Assistant to the Executive Director.

Contents

CHAPTER 1

A Statistical Look at Employment Problems

THE HONORABLE HERBERT BIENSTOCK*

Despite delayed entry into the work place due to increased schooling, and accelerated withdrawal because of early retirement trends, most persons still spend a considerable part of their lives working.

The material that follows is a statistical look at employment problems. It is an attempt to put into perspective problems faced by various segments of the American work force, in particular the under-employed, the over-educated, and the mis-trained.

The first chart [Figure I] presents a quick picture of the economic climate of post-World War II America. It shows the four postwar recessions where unemployment rose to 6 and 7 percent rates—in 1948-1949, 1953-1954, 1958-1959 and 1961-1962. While all the focus was on the peaks of the recessions, it was the recovery periods, indicated by the dashed lines, that were, in

---

*Herbert Bienstock is the Regional Commissioner of Labor Statistics for the U.S. Department of Labor. He has headed the Middle Atlantic Regional Office of the Bureau of Labor Statistics since 1962 and has served in a range of economist positions with the Bureau of Labor Statistics since 1945. He has also taught at Long Island University, Yeshiva University, Cornell University, Baruch and Hunter Colleges of the City University, and the New School. Mr. Bienstock, presently a professor of Labor-Management Relations at Pace University, has written and lectured extensively on labor economic subjects.

Figure I

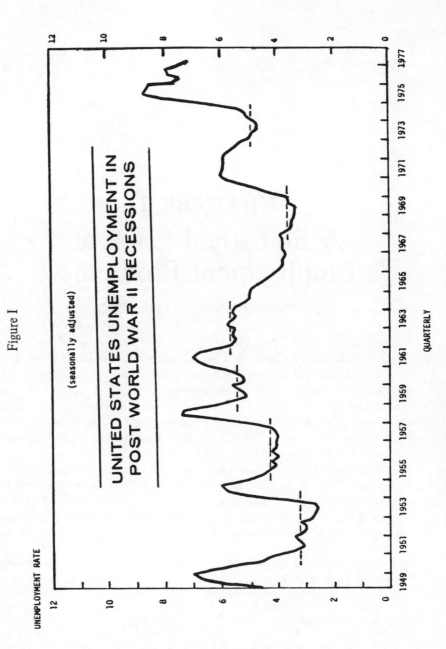

UNEMPLOYMENT RATE

UNITED STATES UNEMPLOYMENT IN
POST WORLD WAR II RECESSIONS

(seasonally adjusted)

QUARTERLY

a way, more significant, especially in terms of the adjustment of people to jobs

Throughout that postwar period, each recovery resulted in rising levels of unemployment. The first dashed line starts out at about the 3.2 percent mark. That is, unemployment fell to 3.2 percent in the recovery following the 1947-1948 recession, but by the time we reach the 1961-1962 recession, the recovery level was up to 5.6 percent. In other words, even when things were booming, more than one out of every 20 Americans was unable to find a job.

After the 1962 recession the "new economics" of Walter Heller took hold. We had tax reductions. In fact, there was a war on poverty. The war on poverty was probably the only war we launched in this country with a tax reduction. But unemployment did begin to drop in 1963 and, by January 1966, it was at the 4 percent mark and it hovered between 3½ and 4 percent right up to 1971. Since then we have had two very serious recessions and we see the last one is still hanging on. It is the deepest one and gives every promise of being the longest recession of the entire postwar period.

Why is it that there are so many people in America today having so much difficulty finding a suitable slot in the job market? Let's take a look at who they tend primarily to be [Figure II]. Although, we must be careful about averages; you can drown in a lake with an average depth of six inches if you find the 10-foot hole.

In the third quarter of 1976, the average unemployment rate was 7.6 percent, but there were also large blocks of people who had a much higher unemployment rate. One could find a 50 percent rate if one wanted to go to poverty areas in ghetto neighborhoods. Blacks and others have been experiencing substantially higher rates of unemployment in this country. Incidentally, that 5 percent rate for white males was the overall rate in the recovery period back in 1961-1962 and 1962-1963. Se we have made some progress, we now have unemployment rates for low-risk groups that equal the average at earlier times for other groups.

The next chart [Figure III] focuses on the hard-core universe of people who are likely to be very good candidates for misfits in industry; because behind unemployment rates lies another group with a much deeper degree of maladjustment in terms of the labor market. To be counted as unemployed in this country, in terms of the methods used, you must be actively seeking a job, it's a labor market concept. We went through that whole Great Depression without having any real measures of unemployment. There was an outfit called the Alexander Hamilton Institute and it used to come out with some private figures, maybe on the basis of the ratio of apples sold or something like that. But, there was no survey until 1938 when a group of unemployed statisticians went to work in a **WPA** program and designed the current household survey method—a concept that is very much grounded in the conditions

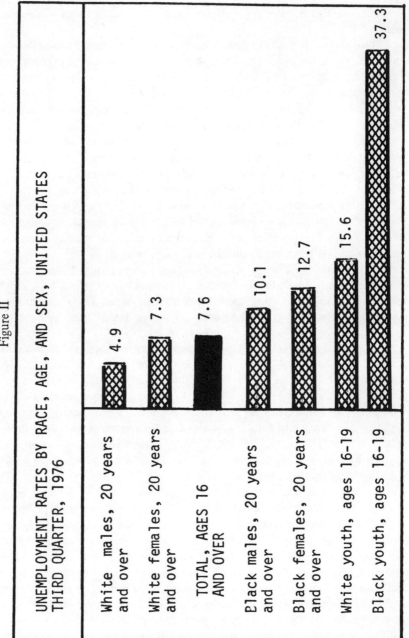

Figure II

UNEMPLOYMENT RATES BY RACE, AGE, AND SEX, UNITED STATES
THIRD QUARTER, 1976

White males, 20 years and over — 4.9

White females, 20 years and over — 7.3

TOTAL, AGES 16 AND OVER — 7.6

Black males, 20 years and over — 10.1

Black females, 20 years and over — 12.7

White youth, ages 16-19 — 15.6

Black youth, ages 16-19 — 37.3

4

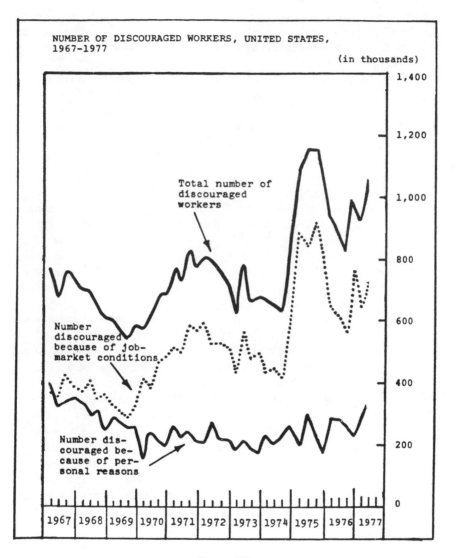

NUMBER OF DISCOURAGED WORKERS, UNITED STATES, 1967–1977

(in thousands)

Total number of discouraged workers

Number discouraged because of job-market conditions

Number discouraged because of personal reasons

1967 1968 1969 1970 1971 1972 1973 1974 1975 1976 1977

Figure III

of the 1930's and that is our labor market concept. If you offer your services in the labor market and those services are not taken, then you are unemployed. So the unemployment rates shown in Figure II relate to people actively seeking employment.

However, Figure III records a very sizable group of people. At the height of the recession, as shown by the top line, there were almost 1,200,000 discouraged workers, workers who do not get counted in the unemployment rate. They are not working, but when there are some further probing questions asked of them, they indicate that if they thought there were jobs readily available, they would be prepared to work. They are not actively seeking employment. They are doing all kinds of other things, keeping house, etc., and simply to count them as unemployed would not make much sense either. The real point is that there were over a million persons only a short time ago, and, if it is any solace, it is down to only 900,000 at last count, who are neither working nor seeking work, but actually not engaged in any other pursuits that would make some optional sense. That is an enormous cadre that really falls into the class of misfits in industry. Perhaps, it is not entirely their fault because clearly the misfit there is part of this dual relationship. The jobs are simply not there for them in a lagging economy.

Figure IV represents another dimension and that is the geographic one. Again we are dealing with averages, and behind every average there lurks a distribution. It is not the same in all parts of the country. We happen to be living in the job disaster part of the country. Inset on the map of the United States is the traditional old industrial crescent of the country, New England, Middle Atlantic, and into the North Central States. Jobs rose over the entire third quarter of the century by only about 37 percent in the industrial tier (E-1) while the Sun Belt, as we are prone to call it for a variety of reasons, that inverted S (E-2), was up by 120 percent.

Even within the Northeast the problems of job accommodation were not the same. Figure V is a picture of the New York-New Jersey area. The top line is for the country as a whole. In 1969-1971, we had a recession in this country. The number of unemployed rose, while employment continued to grow. As a result, we had a very large growth in our labor force. This past year we had the same kind of phenomenon. We added almost three million jobs in this country but we didn't bring the unemployment rate down by anything more than an insignificant notch. From 1971-1974 there were eight million jobs added around the country while employment in New York City declined substantially. The New York-Northeastern New Jersey area had moved up very moderately, but as soon as we got to the last recession, it also fell. We did have a slow recovery in the New York-Northeastern New Jersey area, but in New York City there was no recovery at all.

Basically, we seem to have achieved a long sought objective of eliminating

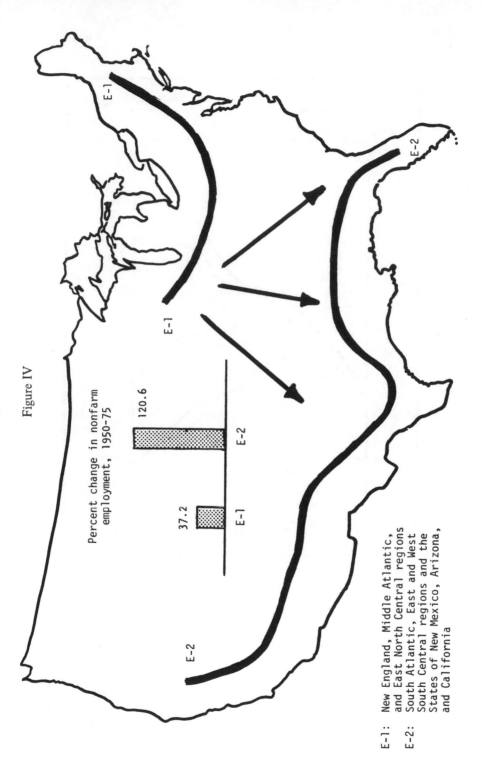

Figure IV

Percent change in nonfarm
employment, 1950-75

120.6

37.2

E-1

E-2

E-1: New England, Middle Atlantic,
      and East North Central regions
E-2: South Atlantic, East and West
      South Central regions and the
      States of New Mexico, Arizona,
      and California

7

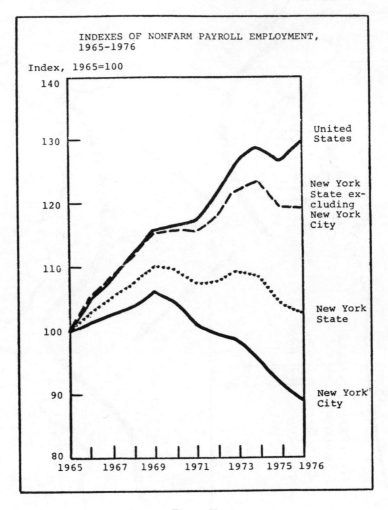

INDEXES OF NONFARM PAYROLL EMPLOYMENT, 1965-1976

Index, 1965=100

United States

New York State excluding New York City

New York State

New York City

Figure V

the business cycle in this part of the country; however, all we have really done is eliminated part of it, the pick-ups. We no longer have recoveries here but we participate fully in the declines. That creates a certain amount of pressure for people in terms of moving elsewhere to find jobs. Figures VI and VII show that this condition continues to persist. This is simply a part of the country in which it becomes increasingly difficult for young people to find a desirable job.

Figure VI
Changes in payroll employment by State, June 1975-November 1976
(numbers in thousands)

State	Total Employment November 1976	Number change June 1975- Nov. 1976	State	Percent change June 1975- Nov. 1976
California.........	8,061.6	206.1	Idaho...........	9.0
Texas	4,575.0	167.5	Utah	8.9
Michigan..........	3,285.1	150.0	Arizona	7.2
Indiana	2,006.3	77.6	Kansas	5.8
Georgia..........	1,778.4	60.6	Wyoming	5.6
Ohio.............	4,107.7	60.4	New Mexico.....	5.5
South Carolina.....	1,028.4	53.8	North Dakota....	5.5
Minnesota........	1,536.5	53.1	South Carolina...	5.5
Arizona..........	760.3	50.8	Mississippi.....	5.3
Virginia	1,809.7	48.4	Nevada.........	5.2
Alabama	1,194.3	47.1	Arkansas	4.9
Missouri..........	1,772.0	46.4	Oregon	4.9
Kansas	840.8	46.1	Michigan	4.8
Wisconsin........	1,724.4	44.7	New Hampshire..	4.6
Oregon	886.7	41.5	Oklahoma.......	4.4
Kentucky..........	1,081.7	40.9	Alabama........	4.1
Utah..............	481.0	39.5	Indiana	4.0
Oklahoma.........	925.9	39.3	Kentucky	3.9
Maryland	1,470.0	38.0	Colorado	3.8
Tennessee	1,531.6	37.3	Texas	3.8
Colorado..........	988.9	35.9	Minnesota	3.6
Mississippi	690.8	34.9	Rhode Island	3.6
Iowa..............	1,029.9	33.6	Georgia	3.5
Illinois	4,476.5	32.9	Iowa	3.4
Washington........	1,262.6	31.5	Vermont........	3.3
Arkansas	648.3	30.0	Nebraska.......	2.8
Louisiana.........	1,216.5	26.7	Maryland	2.7
Idaho.............	300.0	24.8	Missouri	2.7
New Mexico.......	389.9	20.3	Virginia........	2.7
Nebraska	572.8	15.8	Wisconsin	2.7
Nevada	283.2	14.0	California	2.6
New Hampshire....	313.1	13.9	Washington	2.6
West Virginia	575.2	12.7	Tennessee......	2.5
Rhode Island	358.5	12.4	West Virginia ...	2.3
North Dakota......	216.7	11.2	Louisiana.......	2.2
Wyoming..........	161.6	8.6	Delaware	2.0
Florida...........	2,726.3	7.1	Ohio	1.5
North Carolina	1,999.0	6.2	Maine	1.2
Vermont..........	164.2	5.3	South Dakota....	1.1
Delaware	231.6	4.6	Illinois	0.7
Maine	369.4	4.3	Connecticut.....	0.3
New Jersey	2,695.4	3.4	Florida.........	0.3
Connecticut	1,240.3	3.4	North Carolina..	0.3
South Dakota......	216.6	2.4	New Jersey.....	0.1
Montana	247.7	-0.4	Montana........	-0.2
Hawaii............	341.0	-2.7	Pennsylvania....	-0.2
Pennsylvania......	4,437.7	-8.2	Massachusetts ..	-0.5
Alaska............	160.1	-11.2	Hawaii	-0.8
Massachusetts.....	2,320.8	-12.8	New York.......	-1.8
New York.........	6,733.7	-121.3	Alaska	-6.5

Figure VII

Changes in payroll employment, major metropolitan areas,   June 1975-November 1976

(numbers in thousands)

Area	Total Employment November 1976	Number change June 1975- Nov. 1976	Area	Percent change June 1975- Nov. 1976
Detroit...............	1,651.5	78.5	Phoenix..............	8.1
Los Angeles-			Salt Lake City........	7.9
Long Beach	3,102.7	55.4	Anaheim-Santa Ana-	
Houston..............	1,047.7	50.3	Garden Grove.......	7.7
Anaheim-Santa Ana-			San Jose.............	6.0
Garden Grove	620.1	44.5	Portland.............	5.2
Dallas-Fort Worth	1,107.1	34.7	Detroit	5.0
Phoenix..............	453.4	34.1	Houston.............	5.0
San Jose	496.2	28.3	Nashville-Davidson ...	4.8
Chicago..............	3,029.9	25.3	Providence-Warwick-	
Salt Lake City	344.5	25.1	Pawtucket	4.1
Minneapolis-St. Paul..	925.2	24.3	Denver-Boulder	3.8
Portland	464.0	22.9	Greensboro-Winston-	
Denver-Boulder.......	626.0	22.7	Salem-High Pt.	3.7
Atlanta..............	752.6	18.9	Oklahoma City.......	3.7
Baltimore............	864.3	18.8	Sacramento	3.6
Philadelphia..........	1,795.4	18.2	San Diego	3.3
Philadelphia City...	813.2	8.6	Dallas-Fort Worth....	3.2
Washington...........	1,361.2	17.3	Rochester............	3.1
San Diego	487.3	15.5	Columbus	2.8
Providence-Warwick-			New Orleans	2.8
Pawtucket...........	371.6	14.6	Minneapolis-St. Paul..	2.7
Nashville-Davidson....	304.5	14.0	San Antonio	2.7
San Francisco-Oakland.	1,340.1	13.9	Atlanta	2.6
Seattle-Everett	592.3	13.8	Dayton..............	2.5
Kansas City	555.3	12.5	Seattle-Everett.......	2.4
Columbus	460.6	12.4	Kansas City	2.3
Greensboro-Winston-			Baltimore............	2.2
Salem-High Pt.......	337.2	12.1	Memphis.............	2.2
Cleveland	866.9	12.0		
			Los Angeles-	
Rochester............	397.5	12.0	Long Beach.........	1.8
New Orleans..........	429.4	11.8	Buffalo	1.6
Oklahoma City	321.0	11.5	Milwaukee	1.6
St. Louis............	912.5	11.5	Birmingham..........	1.5
Sacramento...........	327.1	11.3	Cleveland............	1.4
Milwaukee............	605.1	9.4		
			Miami	1.4
San Antonio..........	320.1	8.5	Riverside-San	
Dayton	329.3	8.1	Bernardino-Ontario..	1.4
Miami	581.9	8.0	Cincinnati...........	1.3
Buffalo..............	490.0	7.7	St. Louis	1.3
Memphis	324.6	7.1	Washington..........	1.3
Cincinnati............	546.7	6.9		
			Tampa-St. Petersburg.	1.1
Riverside-San			Philadelphia..........	1.0
Bernardino-Ontario..	343.3	4.7	Philadelphia City...	1.1
Birmingham..........	311.6	4.5	SanFrancisco-Oakland.	1.0
Tampa-St. Petersburg.	412.0	4.4	Louisville...........	0.9
Louisville............	351.3	3.1		

(numbers in thousands)

Area	Total Employment November 1976	Number change June 1975– Nov. 1976	Area	Percent change June 1975– Nov. 1976
			Chicago............	0.8
Newark	848.5	1.6	Newark..............	0.2
Boston..............	1,269.3	0.8	Boston..............	0.1
Hartford	339.4	-0.9	Nassau-Suffolk	-0.2
Nassau-Suffolk.......	800.5	-1.4	Hartford.............	-0.3
Indianapolis	449.7	-2.0	Indianapolis	-0.4
Hackensack..........	342.2	-4.1		
			Hackensack	-1.2
Albany-Schenectady-			Albany-Schenectady-	
Troy	303.8	-4.2	Troy...............	-1.4
Pittsburgh............	872.1	-18.3	Pittsburgh	-2.1
New York	3,578.9	-117.3	New York............	-3.2
New York City	3,183.6	-117.0	New York City.....	-3.5

If one looks at the 50 states (Figure VI) during the recovery period from June 1975 to November 1976, the state that has had the least recovery, in fact continues to decline substantially, is New York. Of the 50 largest metropolitan areas shown during the recovery period (Figure VII), others have begun to climb, but the New York area is right down there at the bottom.

What makes for a misfit in industry is literally a misfit between the person and the job. One of the big misfits of the recent past has simply been the lack of available job slots for people to go into. If they haven't fit in, it is because they've been trying to fit into a non-existent situation. Figures VIII, IX, and X show some of the special groups in terms of misfits in industry. Figures VIII and IX are very revealing in terms of understanding the misfits among the black population in this country. We had an enormous migration of blacks from rural south to northern metropolitan areas. The central cities received the bulk of the migration. Although the number of blacks in the suburbs has recently begun to grow, for the most part blacks remain concentrated in the central cities, the places that have had almost nothing in the way of job growth. The central city of New York, for example, has lost 650,000 jobs since 1969. That is more people than are employed in the entire city of Detroit, or the entire Buffalo area.

The move from the rural south also meant a change in employment for black males. In 1940, 41 percent of black males (Figure IX) were working on farm jobs. In contrast, the proportion of black males working as semi-skilled

The Negro population remained close to 10 or 11 percent of the total population between 1900 and 1960, but a shift to the cities did occur.

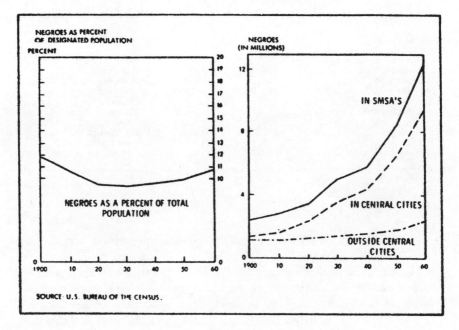

Figure VIII

operatives, i.e., factory workers, was 12 percent. By 1950, as a result of World War II and the enormous manpower shortages that accompanied it, the proportion of black males working on farms dropped from 41 percent in 1940 to 24 percent in 1950 or almost half. The proportion working in the urban factories jumped from 12 to 21 percent, or approximately double, over the same 10-year period. But between 1950 and 1960 the proportion on the farms continued downward as we went through an enormous industrial revolution on those farms. During that period, attention was focused on automation and technology, rather than on the sharp productivity gains that were taking place in the agricultural industry. New machinery made it possible to do a job in minutes that previously had taken hours or weeks. Consequently,

Figure IX

Employed workers age 14 and over (except on Public Emergency Work), by race and sex, United States, 1940, 1950, 1960

Occupation group	Negro						White	
	Male			Female			Male	Female
							1960	1960
	1940	1950	1960(1)	1940	1950	1960(1)		
All occupations: Number (thousands)	2,937	3,501	4,005	1,543	1,875	2,624	39,462	18,549
Percent	100.0	100.0	100.0	100.0	100.0	100.0	100.0	100.0
Professional, technical, and kindred workers	1.7	2.2	3.9	4.2	5.4	7.5	11.0	13.8
Proprietors, managers, and officials, except farm	1.4	2.1	2.3	.7	1.1	1.2	11.5	4.0
Clerks, sales workers	2.6	4.3	6.5	1.4	5.4	10.2	14.5	41.4
Skilled workers, foremen	4.4	7.7	10.2	.1	.6	.7	20.5	1.3
Semiskilled, operatives	11.7	21.0	23.5	13.5	14.6	12.8	19.5	15.7
Unskilled laborers	22.9	23.3	19.4	.8	1.5	1.0	5.6	.5
Service workers	13.7	14.4	14.4	63.4	60.7	55.0	5.3	16.5
Private household	(2)	1.1	.7	(2)	41.8	34.3	.1	4.1
Other	(2)	13.3	13.7	(2)	18.9	20.7	5.2	12.4
Farm workers	41.5	23.7	11.5	15.9	8.9	3.6	7.9	1.4
Farmers, farm managers	21.1	13.4	4.4	3.0	1.7	.7	5.6	.5
Farm laborers	20.4	10.3	7.1	12.9	7.2	2.9	2.3	.9
Occupation not reported	----	1.2	8.4	----	1.6	8.1	4.3	5.3

(1) All nonwhites.
(2) Not available

Source: U.S. Bureau of the Census

13

Figure X

UNEMPLOYMENT RATES OF TEENAGERS (16-19), BY COLOR AND SEX

Annual averages, 1948-1976

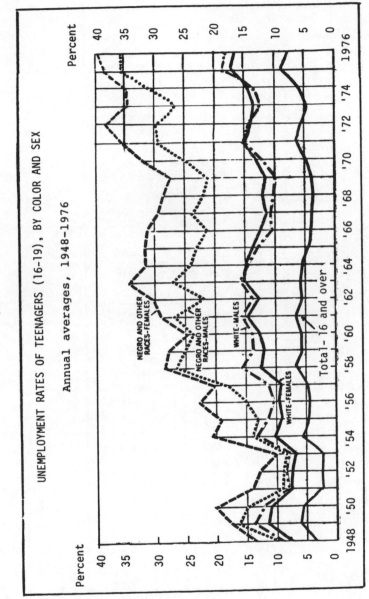

14

the proportions of black males working on farms fell to 11.5 percent. In the brief span of two decades the proportion of black men on farms fell from four in ten to one in ten. On the other hand, there was no compensating growth in factory jobs.

The two major ports of entry into the American labor market for relatively low-skilled people, the farms and the factories, just ground to a halt. Farm employment fell from eight million to three million, while factory employment remained unchanged between 1947 and 1964. There is an easy tendency to feel that this enormous degree of misfit between the black and the American labor market must be the result of something that related to the particular human being. Rather, data like Figure IX suggest that the kind of mobility there was in other periods of time just did not exist during this enormous migration from rural south to urban north.

The young people (Figure X) are another group of misfits. We have almost begun to accept the fact that the unemployment rates for youth must be enormously high and that black minority youngsters must experience rates double that of others. In 1948, unemployment rates for younger people, both black and white, were closely clustered. As each of the postwar recessions (1948-1949, 1953-1954, 1958-1959, 1961-1962 and 1969-1970) made their impact, unemployment rates for teenagers began to spread apart and did not abate during the recoveries. It was this kind of economic climate that brought us to a situation where the unemployment rate during recovery was over 5 percent and those looking for their first job were hit hardest. Clearly, larger and larger numbers were simply not making it. By 1975, the unemployment rate for black youngsters was between 35 and 40 percent and that is the only thing that makes the 18 to 20 percent rate for white youngsters look attractive.

A more pervasive view of discouraged workers can be seen among those who are sub-employed. The latest study, made in November 1966, suggests the degree to which the unemployment rate does not tell very much about socio-economic conditions or the nature of misfits in industry. Between January 1966 and the recession of 1969, the unemployment rate for the United States averaged between 3 and 4 percent. In November 1966, it was 3.4 percent nationwide, but for poverty areas of central cities the rate was markedly higher (Figure XI). But even the 8 percent for Harlem, 9 percent for East Harlem, or 6.2 percent rate for Bedford-Stuyvesant does not give insight into the enormous amount of discombobulation that was taking place in poverty areas of the central cities during that period of the 60's. However, the figure for sub-employment (Figure XII) is a little more indicative. The rate for Harlem was 28.6 percent; East Harlem was 33 percent; and Bedford-Stuyvesant was 27 percent. Those figures represent an estimate of total labor market maladjustment. The three bars in Figure XIII combine the unemploy-

Unemployment rates in poverty areas of selected cities, November 1966

```
United States -------------------------- 3.4%

Boston (Roxbury areas) ----------------- 6.9%
Cleveland (Hough and surrounding
  neighborhood) ----------------------- 15.6%
Detroit (Central Woodward area) -------- 10.1%
Los Angeles (South L.A.) --------------- 12.0%
New Orleans (Several contiguous areas)-- 10.0%
New York:  Harlem ---------------------- 8.1%
           E. Harlem ------------------- 9.0%
           Bedford-Stuyvesant ---------- 6.2%
Oakland (Bayside) ---------------------- 13.0%
Philadelphia (N. Phila.) --------------- 11.0%
Phoenix (Salt River Bed area) ---------- 13.2%
St. Louis (North side) ----------------- 12.9%
San Antonio (East & West sides) -------- 8.1%
San Francisco (Mission-Fillmore) ------- 11.1%
San Juan (El Fanguito) ----------------- 15.8%
```

Figure XI

Sub-employment rate in poverty areas of selected cities, November 1966

Area	Sub-employment rate
Boston ----------------------	24.2%
New Orleans -----------------	45.3%
New York:	
Harlem -----------‑--	28.6%
E. Harlem ---------	33.1%
Bedford-Stuyvesant-	27.6%
Philadelphia ---------------	34.2%
Phoenix --------------------	41.7%
St. Louis ------------------	38.9%
San Antonio ----------------	47.4%
San Francisco --------------	24.6%

Figure XII

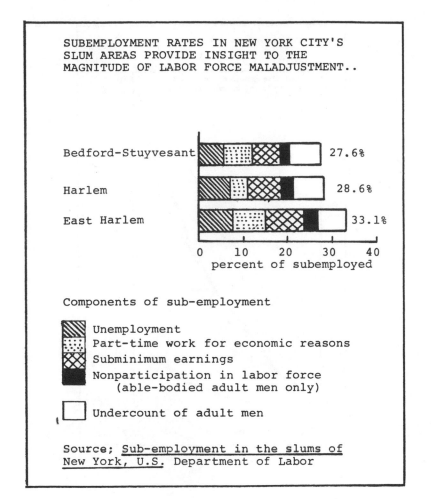

Figure XIII

ment rate with the percentage of people who are working part-time for economic reasons. This group includes people who want more work but are only able to work part-time. Another component of the sub-employed includes workers who receive sub-minimum earnings. This group is made up of people working full-time but clearly not earning enough to reasonably support a family in a high cost area like New York. Added to these groups is the number of adult men who are not counted in the census. On average, an equal number of men and women are born each year, yet a census count in a typi-

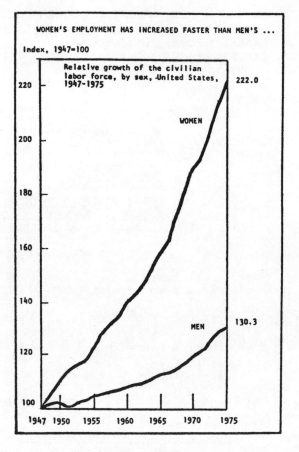

Figure XIV

cal central city poverty area finds 10 percent or so fewer males. The census, while it does not count births, immigration, or deaths is simply a household oriented count that substantially undercounts males who are not in a household-related situation. A sub-employment rate of over 30 or 40 percent gives one a feel for the dimensions of misfits in slum areas.

Misfits in industry are not, however, limited to groups in the so-called "subculture." The issue of working women has also had an impact on work and mental health. Between 1947 and 1975 the number of men in the labor force has increased by about 30 percent while the number of women has increased by 122 percent (Figure XIV). This is somewhat misleading, however, because it counts persons in the labor force and not the total number of

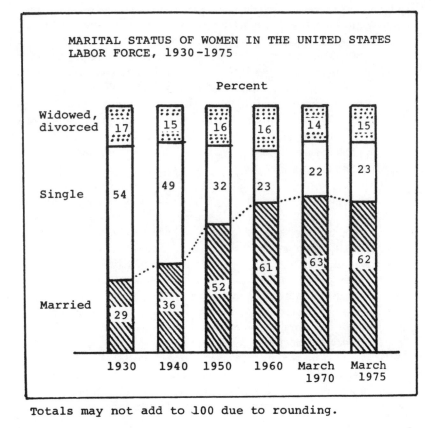

MARITAL STATUS OF WOMEN IN THE UNITED STATES
LABOR FORCE, 1930-1975

Percent

Widowed, divorced: 17, 15, 16, 16, 14, 15

Single: 54, 49, 32, 23, 22, 23

Married: 29, 36, 52, 61, 63, 62

1930   1940   1950   1960   March 1970   March 1975

Totals may not add to 100 due to rounding.

Figure XV

hours worked. For example, on Long Island there has been an enormous shift from high pay, full-time and even overtime jobs in the aircraft plants, largely held by men, to relatively low pay, part-time jobs in shopping centers that are primarily held by women. Whether they are low pay because they are held by women or held by women because they are low pay is a chicken and egg question you can decide for yourself. The point obviously is that a line that counts each person goes up much sharper for women than the line which would show, for example, aggregate work hours or total income.

As of March 1975, almost two-thirds of all women in the American labor market were married (Figure XV). Hence, the dual job pressure of home and job becomes another significant element in regard to mental health and its relationship to work. Bear in mind that despite recent social changes concerning working women, most still work because of economic need. As a corollary to the dramatic rise of married women in the labor force, we now find 27,619,000 children under the age of 18 who live in households with a working mother (Figure XVI). That is equivalent to one out of eight Americans. Even more startling than this figure is the 6.5 million youngsters under the age of six who live in a household with a working mother. This may not be a frightening fact by itself, but clearly not every family is able to afford the care that children under six generally require when the mother is at work. Are we prepared institutionally to deal with the implications this has now or may have in the future?

Obviously, it is illusions that create frustrations. In the work place, one example is in terms of earnings, gross versus "real" spendable income. The "grand illusion" (Figure XVII) has been the sharp rise in average weekly earnings for the typical production worker in the United States. (A similar kind of relationship would also hold true for other groups of workers.) Because average weekly factory earnings rose from $107 in 1965 to $189 in 1975, a worker feels that he is making more. Yet, when that worker spends his higher paycheck, he finds that while $107 in 1965 had a "real" spendable value of $88, 10 years later it can still only buy about $84 worth of goods and services. Incidentally, the only year he made any advances was between 1972-73 when we had a wage-price freeze.

While inflation and its attendant earnings illusion have a severe impact on mental health in the work place, unemployment has other significant implications. For some, being out of work means not looking for a job and simply leaving the labor force. They move into that discouraged worker group, no longer counted as unemployed. In 1975, among persons aged 60 and over, (Figure XVIII), 60 percent of the men and 65 percent of the women who left unemployment did so by leaving the labor force.

The enormous change in the nature of work and the kind of jobs that are around today is also responsible for creating more and more misfits in industry. The basic long-term trends by industry (Figure XIX) show service producing industries as being the sectors with the most rapid growth. While the implications for future training are apparent, the implications for mental health are more subtle. Industries where something tangible is produced, like the construction of a house, the extraction of ore, the manufacture of a product, or the production of a food, are no longer the areas in which jobs are growing.

Additionally, in September 1976, we finally penetrated the 50 percent mark in terms of white-collar jobs as a proportion of all occupations in this country (Figure XX). Since the early 50's, white-collar jobs have been rising more rapidly than blue-collar jobs, but that comparison tends to leave out a

Figure XVI

Number of children under 18 years old, by age, type of family, labor force
status of mother, and race, March 1975

(numbers in thousands)

Item	Age of children, 1975		
	Under 18 years	Under 6 years	6 to 17 years
Total children -------------	62,725	18,150	44,575
Mother in labor force -------------	27,619	6,538	21,081
Mother not in labor force -------------	34,213	11,481	22,732
Husband-wife families -------------	52,611	15,687	36,924
Mother in labor force -------------	22,595	5,439	17,155
Mother not in labor force -------------	30,016	10,248	19,769
Female family head -------------	9,221	2,333	6,389
Mother in labor force -------------	5,024	1,099	3,925
Mother not in labor force -------------	4,197	1,234	2,963
Other male family head -------------	892	130	762

Figure XVII

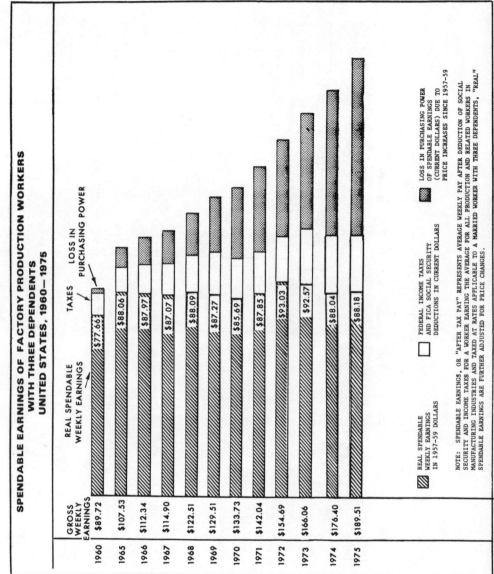

SPENDABLE EARNINGS OF FACTORY PRODUCTION WORKERS
WITH THREE DEPENDENTS
UNITED STATES, 1960—1975

	GROSS WEEKLY EARNINGS	REAL SPENDABLE WEEKLY EARNINGS IN 1957-59 DOLLARS
1960	$89.72	$77.66
1965	$107.53	$88.06
1966	$112.34	$87.97
1967	$114.90	$87.07
1968	$122.51	$88.09
1969	$129.51	$87.27
1970	$133.73	$85.69
1971	$142.04	$87.85
1972	$154.69	$93.03
1973	$166.06	$92.57
1974	$176.40	$88.04
1975	$189.51	$88.18

Legend:
- REAL SPENDABLE WEEKLY EARNINGS IN 1957-59 DOLLARS
- FEDERAL INCOME TAXES AND FICA SOCIAL SECURITY DEDUCTIONS IN CURRENT DOLLARS
- LOSS IN PURCHASING POWER OF SPENDABLE EARNINGS (CURRENT DOLLARS) DUE TO PRICE INCREASES SINCE 1957-59

NOTE: SPENDABLE EARNINGS, OR "AFTER TAX PAY" REPRESENTS AVERAGE WEEKLY PAY AFTER DEDUCTION OF SOCIAL SECURITY AND INCOME TAXES FOR A WORKER EARNING THE AVERAGE FOR ALL PRODUCTION AND RELATED WORKERS IN MANUFACTURING INDUSTRIES AND TAXED AT RATES APPLICABLE TO A MARRIED WORKER WITH THREE DEPENDENTS, "REAL" SPENDABLE EARNINGS ARE FURTHER ADJUSTED FOR PRICE CHANGES.

22

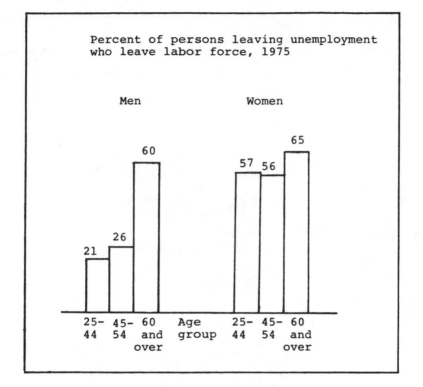

Figure XVIII

very large component, service and farm jobs. Considering all categories of work, we are now a white-collar society (Figure XXI). The issue is, are workers geared for that society?

An understanding of the aggregate of the misfit can be gathered from looking at the percent distribution of unemployment and projected job openings by occupation as shown in Figure XXI. Thirty-four percent of all unemployed persons in 1976 had held white-collar type jobs. Yet, this category should account for close to 60 percent of the projected openings, or about double the percentage of unemployed. On the other hand, the 48 percent of the unemployed whose last job was a blue-collar type, were seeking a job where only about 20 percent of the projected job openings are expected to be found. The blue-collar group thus epitomizes misfits in industry.

However, there is a bright note. Although we may not have rapid growth,

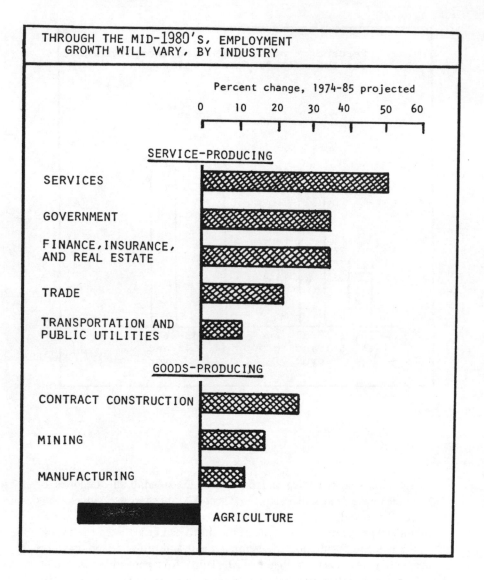

THROUGH THE MID-1980's, EMPLOYMENT
GROWTH WILL VARY, BY INDUSTRY

Percent change, 1974-85 projected

SERVICE-PRODUCING

SERVICES

GOVERNMENT

FINANCE, INSURANCE,
AND REAL ESTATE

TRADE

TRANSPORTATION AND
PUBLIC UTILITIES

GOODS-PRODUCING

CONTRACT CONSTRUCTION

MINING

MANUFACTURING

AGRICULTURE

Figure XX

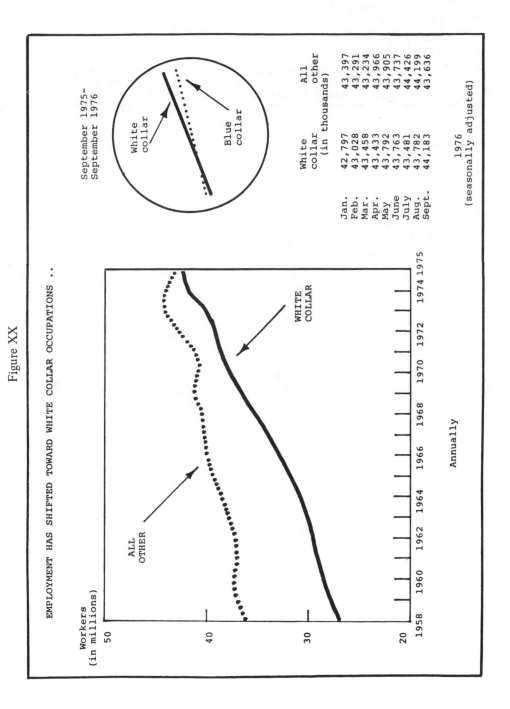

EMPLOYMENT HAS SHIFTED TOWARD WHITE COLLAR OCCUPATIONS ..

Workers
(in millions)

September 1975-
September 1976

White collar

Blue collar

	White collar	All other
	(in thousands)	
Jan.	42,797	43,397
Feb.	43,028	43,291
Mar.	43,458	43,234
Apr.	43,433	43,966
May	43,792	43,905
June	43,763	43,737
July	43,481	44,426
Aug.	43,782	44,199
Sept.	44,183	43,636

1976
(seasonally adjusted)

WHITE COLLAR

ALL OTHER

1958 1960 1962 1964 1966 1968 1970 1972 1974 1975

Annually

50
40
30
20

Figure XXI

Percent distribution by occupational group of nonfarm employed and unemployed with prior work experience of last job, 1976 and projected job
openings 1974-85, United States

Group	1976		Projected job openings 1974-85
	Unem- ployed	Em- ployed	
Total----------------------------	100.0	100.0	100.0
White collar workers ------------	33.6	51.6	59.3
Professional and technical workers --------------------	7.0	15.7	16.3
Managers and administrators ---	4.7	11.0	9.0
Salesworkers ------------------	5.0	6.5	5.9
Clerical workers --------------	16.9	18.4	28.2
Blue collar workers -------------	48.0	34.2	21.6
Craft and kindred workers -----	13.3	13.3	8.8
Operatives --------------------	23.8	15.8	10.4
Nonfarm laborers --------------	10.9	5.1	2.4
Service workers -----------------	18.4	14.2	19.0

there still will be an enormous number of job openings due to replacement
in blue-collar occupations. In fact, most job openings in all categories of jobs
develop because somebody dies or retires and has to be replaced. Between
1974 and 1985 (Figure XXII), it is expected that there will be 57,600,000
job openings in this country. While growth should account for only about 17
million, the remainder will stem from replacement needs. It was not too long
ago that Henry Wallace wrote a book called "60 Million Jobs" and people
laughed him out of court. Today we are predicting almost 60 million job
openings and a total employment of more than 100 million.

In recent years we have found that some of our higher echelon workers,
college graduates, professionals and technical workers, can also be misfits.
Since 1969, the unemployment rate for professional and technical workers
began to rise more rapidly than for the labor market as a whole. Although
most college graduates still find employment as professional and technical
workers or managers and administrators, beginning in 1969, college graduates
had a harder time finding these jobs. This difficulty, for the most part, was
due to the fact that supply and demand were coming into line with each
other (Figure XXIII). There was no significant slackening of demand for
college graduates as some have suggested. In fact, during the last recession
(1974-75) when we lost two million blue-collar jobs, professional and technical and managerial and administrative positions continued to grow by three
quarters of a million. It is true that unemployment among college graduates

Figure XXII

Projected Employment Growth by Major Occupational Group, 1974–85
(In thousands)

Occupational Group	1974 Employment	Projected 1985 Employment	Percent Change	Openings		
				Total	Growth	Replacements
Total	85,936	103,400	20.3	57,600	17,400	40,200
White-collar workers	41,739	53,200	27.5	34,300	11,500	22,800
Professional and technical workers	12,338	16,000	29.4	9,400	3,600	5,700
Managers and administrators	8,941	10,900	21.6	5,200	1,900	3,200
Salesworkers	5,417	6,300	15.7	3,400	900	2,600
Clerical workers	15,043	20,100	33.8	16,300	5,100	11,300
Blue-collar workers	29,776	33,700	13.2	12,500	3,900	8,600
Craft and kindred workers	11,477	13,800	19.9	5,100	2,300	2,800
Operatives¹	13,919	15,200	9.0	6,000	1,300	4,800
Nonfarm laborers	4,380	4,800	8.8	1,400	400	1,100
Service workers	11,373	14,600	28.0	11,000	3,200	7,800
Farm workers	3,048	1,900	–39.0	–200	–1,200	1,000

¹ Includes the 1970 Census classification: operatives, except transport and transport equipment operatives.

Note: Details may not add to totals because of rounding.

27

Figure XXIII

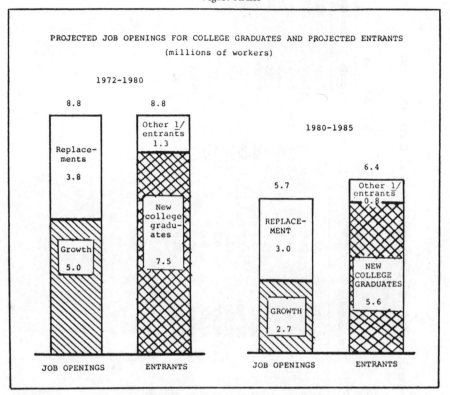

PROJECTED JOB OPENINGS FOR COLLEGE GRADUATES AND PROJECTED ENTRANTS
(millions of workers)

1972-1980

8.8   8.8

Replace-
ments
3.8   Other 1/
                   entrants
                   1.3

Growth   New
5.0   college
           gradu-
           ates
           7.5

1980-1985

5.7   6.4

REPLACE-   Other 1/
MENT   entrants
3.0   0.8

            NEW
GROWTH   COLLEGE
2.7   GRADUATES
            5.6

JOB OPENINGS   ENTRANTS   JOB OPENINGS   ENTRANTS

1/ Includes reentrants, delayed entrants, immigrants, and military separations.

did rise to 2.8 percent (Figure XXIV) from the 1.8 and 1.9 rate that they enjoyed in the halcyon days of the 1950's and 60's. Still, that rate is well below the March 1976 average of 8 percent for all workers. Until about 1969, companies would recruit college graduates and carry them off on a magic carpet because they were in short supply and companies were stuck hiring brainpower. But by 1969 the crop of post-World War II babies began graduating from college and poured into the labor market, upsetting the supply and demand relationship for graduates that had existed.

In fact, the American labor market has really been dominated by the post-war baby crop. Born in 1947, they began elementary school in 1953. By 1963, at age 16 they hit the American labor market as dropouts right at the end of the fourth postwar recession. The labor market was not waiting with open arms for high school dropouts, and the teenage unemployment rates

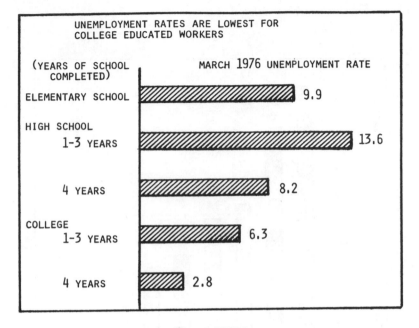

UNEMPLOYMENT RATES ARE LOWEST FOR
COLLEGE EDUCATED WORKERS

(YEARS OF SCHOOL
COMPLETED)

MARCH 1976 UNEMPLOYMENT RATE

ELEMENTARY SCHOOL — 9.9

HIGH SCHOOL
1-3 YEARS — 13.6

4 YEARS — 8.2

COLLEGE
1-3 YEARS — 6.3

4 YEARS — 2.8

Figure XXIV

soared to the 18 and 20 percent mark with all the attendant impacts in terms of mental health. Those who went to college in 1965 and graduated in 1969 suddenly found that supply and demand was in a tight relationship for highly educated workers. It wasn't that demand was letting up, rather supply was increasing as a result of enrollments soaring from two million to ten million.

There are some better days ahead, however. Most notably, the 1947 youngsters have now reached the age of 30 and for the next 15 years or so they are going to be passing through a less dependent period than when they were under 30. Ages 30 to 45 tend to be a period of high production and high consumption. In fact, the demographic signals for the years ahead are distinctly on the plus side. At the present time, however, some recent college graduates continue to be plagued by high rates of unemployment (Figure XXV). Social science and humanities graduates with rates of 15 and 16 percent are still examples of hard-core misfits. Another very substantial concern, besides the degree to which graduates do not find employment, is the degree of job dissatisfaction when they do find a job. Figure XXVI shows that 43 percent of the humanities majors and over 54 percent of the social science majors wind up at work that is in no way related to their fields of study. The

Figure XXV

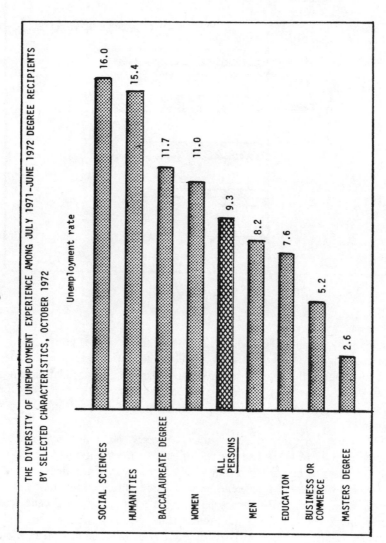

THE DIVERSITY OF UNEMPLOYMENT EXPERIENCE AMONG JULY 1971-JUNE 1972 DEGREE RECIPIENTS
BY SELECTED CHARACTERISTICS, OCTOBER 1972

Unemployment rate

SOCIAL SCIENCES   16.0
HUMANITIES   15.4
BACCALAUREATE DEGREE   11.7
WOMEN   11.0
ALL PERSONS   9.3
MEN   8.2
EDUCATION   7.6
BUSINESS OR COMMERCE   5.2
MASTERS DEGREE   2.6

Figure XXVI   Relationship of work of degree recipients 1/ to major field of study and reason for working in a job not directly related to field, by selected characteristics, October 1972

(Percent distribution)

Relationship and reason	Total	Sex		Type of degree		Major field of study				
		Men	Women	Bachelor's	All other	Business or commerce	Education	Social sciences	Humanities	All other
RELATIONSHIP OF WORK TO FIELD										
Total employed: Number (thousands)	666	399	266	471	195	105	204	97	77	183
Percent	100.0	100.0	100.0	100.0	100.0	100.0	100.0	100.0	100.0	100.0
Directly related	68.5	66.1	71.4	61.3	86.3	61.5	81.9	45.8	56.2	74.7
Used much of training	52.4	45.9	61.3	43.9	73.2	27.9	71.9	29.2	47.9	58.8
Used some of training	16.2	20.2	10.2	17.4	13.2	33.7	10.0	16.7	8.2	15.9
Not directly related	31.4	33.9	28.6	38.7	13.7	38.5	18.1	54.2	43.8	25.3
Used some of training	12.2	13.8	10.5	14.4	6.8	26.0	6.5	20.8	9.6	7.1
Used little or none of training	19.2	20.2	18.0	24.3	6.8	12.5	11.6	33.3	34.2	18.1
Somewhat related	13.0	14.0	12.0	15.3	7.4	24.0	7.0	25.0	12.3	7.1
Used some of training	9.2	10.2	8.3	10.5	5.8	19.2	6.0	16.7	6.8	3.8
Used little or none of training	3.8	3.8	3.8	4.7	1.6	4.8	1.0	8.3	5.5	3.3
Not related	18.5	19.9	16.5	23.4	6.3	14.4	11.1	29.2	31.5	18.1
Used some of training	3.1	3.6	2.3	3.9	1.1	6.7	.5	4.2	2.7	3.3
Used little or none of training	15.4	16.3	14.3	19.6	5.3	7.7	10.6	25.0	28.8	14.8
MAIN REASON FOR WORK NOT DIRECTLY RELATED										
Not directly related: Number (thousands)	210	135	76	182	27	40	37	53	34	46
Percent	100.0	100.0	100.0	100.0	(2/)	(2/)	(2/)	(2/)	(2/)	(2/)
Could not find job in field	49.3	43.1	61.1	48.0	-	-	-	-	-	-
Better pay than in major field	6.5	7.7	4.2	7.3	-	-	-	-	-	-
Better opportunity for advancement than in major field	8.0	9.2	5.6	7.3	-	-	-	-	-	-
To see if liked kind of work	8.0	9.2	5.6	7.8	-	-	-	-	-	-
Did not want to work in field	5.5	6.2	4.2	6.1	-	-	-	-	-	-
All other	22.9	24.6	19.4	23.5	-	-	-	-	-	-

1/ See footnote 1, table 1.
2/ Percent not shown where base is less than 75,000.

31

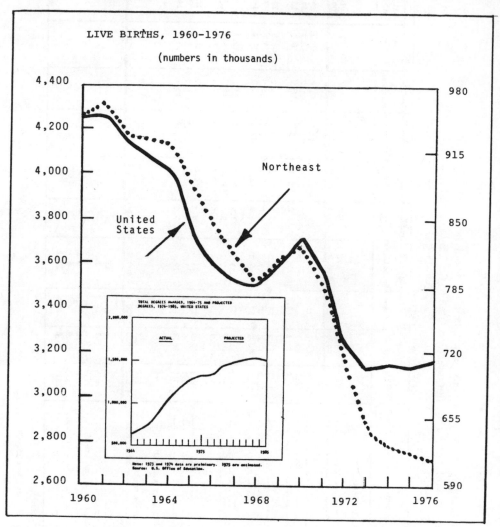

LIVE BIRTHS, 1960–1976

(numbers in thousands)

Source: Life births data are from the Department of Health, Education and Welfare.

Figure XXVII

implications of that in terms of mental health must be substantial.

However, there are already a set of factors in process that should lead to an improved environment for dealing with these issues. The basis for this optimism is the dramatic decline in live births in this country since 1960 (Figure XXVII). The postwar baby crop is now passing out of the picture very substantially, except as consumers. Although 5 or 6 percent of that crop still have employment problems, most of the group has now been absorbed into the labor market. Now, another group dominates the American scene and that is the group that was not born in the 1960's. Nationally, the birth rate dropped from four million a year to three million a year, the same level that we had in 1946 before the postwar baby boom. And while the numbers are now at the same level as in 1946, they are coming into a population that is much larger.

Hence, we should be entering a period of manpower shortages. With all the technological advances we have made, one thing we have not figured out is how to produce a 20-year-old in less than 20 years. While we cannot accurately forecast the inflation rate or the unemployment rate, we can predict with enormous certainty those people who will not be around in the middle 80's. What is more, the kids who were not born in 1960 will not be graduating from college in 1982 and therefore, the number of college graduates should level off. This leveling off in a knowledge society such as ours, accompanied by increasing demand for highly educated workers, suggests inevitable manpower shortages beginning in the 1980's.

In conclusion, this new set of supply-and-demand relationships coming up will make it more feasible to deal with the issue and problems of misfits. When you throw grass on a concrete sidewalk, you don't have a chance of getting a decent lawn. If you throw it on a pliable, well-worked piece of earth there is no guarantee you are going to get a good lawn either, but your chances are substantially improved. This, therefore, is the time to be concerned with problems like misfits in industry because, at best they may just be more manageable in the years ahead.

DISCUSSION

Panelists included:

Joseph Barbaro, C.S.W., Executive Director, Catholic Charities, Diocese of Rockville Centre

Vicki Moss, Counselor, "Women Working," A Federally Funded Project for Unemployed and Under-employed Women

William Sims, M.A., Placement Coordinator, The Rehabilitation Center

Frederick Snyder, M.Phil., Ph.D., J.D., Graduate Fellow, Harvard Law School

Dr. Snyder:

Before I went to law school six years ago, and after graduation from college, I worked for two years at a large industrial corporation in New York and, at various times during that period, I was alternately an over-qualified, mis-matched, mis-trained and under-trained employee.

Mr. Sims:

I am the job developer for The Rehabilitation Institute (TRI), the first facility of its kind on Long Island to serve the emotionally handicapped and discharged mental hospital patients. We serve individuals aged 16 and up (a recent job placement was a man of 64), by providing vocational training, workshop activities, and job evaluation and placement. Our average daily census is around 245.

TRI's 14 vocational training courses in industrial, clerical, and food service skills are approved by the New York State Education Department. Our workshop maintains the individual in the community and provides paid employment on a piece-rate basis in a protective work setting. Subcontracts from local commerce and industry offer actual working conditions.

TRI's clinical services, including group and individual counseling, and family casework, support our vocational training emphasis.

We are supported by public contributions and grants, and all services are provided at no cost to the client.

Mr. Barbaro:

We just employed one of your people. He was a volunteer with us for a couple of months. After the papers went through, we hired him. He has worked out fine.

Ms. Moss:

I am part of a team that is developing a project that has been funded by the Department of Labor, under the Comprehensive Employment and Training Act (CETA). Title III of CETA pertains to specific segments of the population. My specific segment is women. We are one of 30 such programs across the country set up to meet the specific employability needs of women which are, in many cases, different from the needs of men.

Mr. Sims:

I believe that if a psychiatric center is going to be successful, it really should develop a professional placement service. I am a salesman; I try to convince firms to hire the emotionally restored. The success of my referrals depends on a complete job description, knowledge of the type of supervision that our client will have to deal with, and overall honesty.

Audience:

Could you tell us something about the type of people that TRI serves?

Mr. Sims:

Most of our people are emotionally handicapped. They come to us, through the New York State Division of Vocational Rehabilitation, from community agencies, mental health practitioners, and hospitals. Some come to us after acute psychotic breaks. Some are chronic schizophrenics. Some are able to function well when they come to us, while others need resocialization.

Audience:

What if an individual doesn't want to take the job you offer?

Mr. Sims:

We do not insist that the client take any job that is offered. The applicant is given the facts about the job, options are evaluated; if there is still no interest, we stop. We tell our clients that job seeking will continue and that they will be informed when suitable jobs become available.

Audience:

I know how extremely difficult it is to convince people to take on people who have had a psychiatric history. Thirty years ago, as a mental hygiene worker, I struggled alone to try to place our patients, with very little success. Your program makes me feel optimistic about progress.

Audience:

I'd like to know more about government programs now underway for the disadvantaged and disabled.

Ms. Moss:

CETA is the Comprehensive Employment and Training Act, passed in 1973. There are a number of programs funded under CETA which are designed to train people who are unemployed or under-employed. In some instances, jobs are found where people can be trained right on the job. CETA funds some of these jobs, either fully or partially, for a certain period of time. There are work experience positions which are usually four-month jobs, half-funded by the CETA program and half-funded by the employer. This gets people used to being in the work force and used to working in certain fields. CETA also sends people to technical schools to acquire new skills.

Under Title I, people can be in a CETA program up to two years. In my particular program, which is under Title III, we are funded only for a year, so we are looking for training programs that are rather short-term.

In my program, designed especially for women, we have people in para-legal programs, people studying to become computer programmers, people training to be computer repairwomen. We have some women training on the job, learning to sell large appliances and automobiles, which is rather unusual. We are aiming to place women in so-called non-traditional jobs, in slots that are not at present filled by women.

Audience:

CETA also provides funds for training people in work habits. Many people, especially the young, have little or no work experience. CETA will also provide funds for people to learn basic arithmetic and English.

Audience:

I would like to know what kind of effort is being made to place the unemployed middle-aged worker.

Ms. Moss:

The program that I am with is certainly addressing this problem, be-cause so many of the women who come into our program are women who have been out of the work force for 15 or 20 years. They have been working as unpaid laborers in the homes and have been acquiring skills that have not been recognized as marketable.

Audience:

I would like to know the distinction between CETA and OVR, the Office of Vocational Rehabilitation, and the kind of formal relationship they have.

Ms. Moss:

We try not to duplicate, but rather to cooperate. We refer people to the Department of Vocational Rehabilitation when we feel that their services are needed for people who have disabilities that require medical or psychiatric care. They, in turn, refer people to us when we have suitable jobs in which to place people.

Audience:

Our agency gets many requests for a homemaker, and there just aren't any. For instance, I know a woman who needs to go for treatment two times a week. Her husband is a roofer, but he will lose his job if he has to continue taking time off to take his wife to the hospital. The union called me and asked me to find somebody to take his wife for treatment. There is nobody I can find who will take two mornings off on a long-term basis. It's sad.

Mr. Barbaro:

One of the Homemaker Services on Long Island has some grant money and a union local gave them space. They are training people who want to do that kind of work. It certainly is going to meet a need.

Audience:

Ms. Moss, how do you help the women in your program?

Ms. Moss:

To be eligible for our program, a woman must be an unemployed resident of our county (Bergen County, N.J.). She can come in any time to see an intake specialist who takes down relevant information and sets up an appointment with a counselor. The counselor assesses the woman's employment needs in terms of the clarity of her goals and the kinds of skills she needs to attain these goals.

For those who require help in deciding what they want, we run group workshops. We also teach interviewing techniques and resume writing skills in workshop situations. For low-income women, we have funding for training.

We have job developers who scout the area for all sorts of positions, and we have a placement counselor who works with women who are ready to go right out and job hunt. We also run what we call a "job club" for women who are involved in the job hunt. These women meet twice a week to structure their activities, to discuss problems, and to give one another support. We have had a high success rate with women in the job club.

As I said before, we are trying to emphasize non-traditional job categories where women are not represented very highly. Women are very well represented in the teaching field, in social work, in nursing, and in clerical jobs. More and more women will be entering the job market in this decade. When you think of the number of jobs available in those categories I just named, you'll realize that these areas will become saturated. We have to get women into new areas.

Audience:

There are women who really would prefer to do homemaking. They don't really want to compete with men in the business world. There is a great need for them as professional homemakers. But, when it comes down to finding a particular homemaker for a particular patient, we have a dreadfully hard time. I have tried over and over again, with no success. There is such a pressing need for homemaker services.

Do you encourage women to work as homemakers or do you stress other types of jobs?

Ms. Moss:

We don't coerce anyone. If a woman wants to work as a visiting home-maker, we'll try to help her.

Audience:

The program that you are involved in and other such programs are mush-rooming. Do you feel the vast sums of money being spent are warranted in view of the fact that the market is saturated already?

Ms. Moss:

What I said was that the market was saturated with secretaries, teachers, social workers, so-called female positions, and we are trying to help women realize that they can do other kinds of work where the market is not satur-ated.

Audience:

Is that the way you see the future?

Ms. Moss:

To have women do other kinds of work? Sure, I hope.

Audience:

The labor force is calculated by participation rate. Participation rate is those aged 16 or over in the population looking for, or seeking, employment. Now participation rates in this country have stayed at 60 percent, plus or minus, for 25 years. We have seen a tremendous increase in the participation rate of women; but what everyone is refusing to admit is that we have a tre-mendous decline in the participation rate of men. Unemployment wouldn't be what it is if the participation labor of women were what it was 25 years ago.

Ms. Moss:

The majority of working women work out of need, not because they are bored at home, but because they need the money. Many, many of them are supporting families; many are the sole support of their families, and they need the money to support their families just as men do. That is another reason we would like to get them into so-called non-traditional jobs, because they pay better.

Audience:

Are the people trained by these programs expected to perform at the same level as the other workers in a company?

Mr. Barbaro:

If they are signed in as trainees, then the expectation is not that they are going to be at the same level. But, over a period of time, they must meet a standard equal to the others. For instance, when they start, they may be able to type only 30 words a minute but, by the end of that six-month period, they should be able to type 50 words per minute if that is the standard.

Audience:

If I get a worker through a Federally funded program and he is a dud, am I stuck with him?

Mr. Barbaro:

First of all, there is a selection process. We interview the people and select those whom we think have the skills and the personality and the motivation to fit the jobs and then there are periodic evaluations. If problems develop, the worker can be dropped.

Ms. Moss:

We do screening and we try to send people to employment situations where their skills match the request. Aside from our screening, the places that we try to place people in also interview them just as they would any other candidate for a job.

Audience:

I think the basic principle which applies to most rehab programs is that the person has to be a potential worker; otherwise you spoil your credibility.

Ms. Moss:

Absolutely.

Audience:

There is a morale factor involved for people who are productive employees if they see someone less experienced being trained, presumably to do the same type of job, and that person is not performing.

Audience:

The expectations of the employer do not seem to be the same as they would be for another type of employee.

Ms. Moss:

They should be the same.

Audience:

The staff has to know that people are coming in as trainees.

Audience:

I think that is the secret.

Mr. Sims:

Before we referred anyone to Catholic Charities we knew exactly what they needed and we knew the background. In order for us to open up future possibilities at Catholic Charities, we had to be exceptionally careful to get the right combination going.

Audience:

About 99 percent of the people in private industry are not interested in the handicapped and, until this attitude is changed, what are we going to do with these so-called misfits? One percent of private industry cannot employ all of them.

Mr. Sims:

Any private firm that does business with government actually has to hire some handicapped persons.

Audience:

Half of the people who are unemployed are people who have some disability, either physical or mental. This is the area that we should concentrate on.

Audience:

There are models in other countries that are extremely effective. England has models that have very large contracts with various industries or factories. They employ people who can go up and down the ladder, according to their capabilities. There are villages in Holland where a whole community is geared to helping the handicapped. They bring in special industry and it is partially subsidized.

Dr. Snyder:

I'd like to pick up on one of the themes of Mr. Bienstock's speech. He stated, for example, that unemployment rates for the past four or five years are low for workers who have gone to college: the demand for college graduates today is three times greater than for other members of the work force. Yet 30 percent of the college graduates employed in industrial corporations are employed in jobs that have no direct correlation to their academic courses of study. In addition, 31.4 percent of the persons who have humanities and social science degrees are currently unemployed or under-employed.

Now, the idea that a person with a liberal arts education doesn't know anything useful for industrial purposes is nothing new. In the past, industrial organizations simply retrained, or trained anew, persons who were well educated but "unskilled." This was a luxury that industry could well afford, in return for the prestige of having college-educated personnel on its staff. We were in a growth economy until the early 1970's. Plants were being built at a rapid rate; product lines were diversifying at a rapid rate. From all appearances, however, it seems that the period of accelerated growth of the large industrial organization in this country is at an end, and that the day of the slow-growth economy is upon us.

American industry is still engaged in "capital-intensive" efforts, of course, but more in foreign markets than at home. In the underdeveloped countries, for instance, demand for even the simplest products is high, labor is cheap, and raw materials are in plentiful supply. It makes sense to build and expand in such areas. There, too, one need not face the problem of plowing vast sums of money into the retraining of liberal arts college graduates; skill-training programs are generally part of the package the industry works out with the government of the country in which it is investing.

In light of these global developments, it might be a good idea for us all to take a wholly new look at college education in this country, at our concepts of what a college education is and what it can provide. In the early decades of this century, you will recall, a college education was perceived as a privilege of the few. For the past 20 years or so we have toyed with the idea of a college education as the right of all.

Perhaps today we should take a more balanced view and begin looking at education as a commodity that can be purchased and used by its consumers when, and as, they need it. Maybe some form of continuing adult education ought to serve as a model for the dominant form of undergraduate college education in the future. The bulk of government financial aid might be made available to adults, for example, who are already working, to help them free up their time to choose educational programs which suit their evolving employment needs. This, of course, represents a fundamental change in the concept of a liberal college education in America. But if there is a need for such structural change in the way college education relates to job needs, that change will surely take place.

CHAPTER 2
Some Psychiatric Aspects of Mis-Employment

ROBERT L. MEINEKER, M.D.*

Employment problems in industry arise from many sources, ranging from economic and political to climatic and geographical. Many of them stem from situations quite beyond the scope of psychiatry. However, in instances where a person's abilities, personality, or motivations don't meet the requirements of the job or mesh with the personalities of those who operate it, psychiatry, psychology, and sociology may provide some useful insights and remedies.

As you can see, I have included psychology and sociology, along with psychiatry, as sources of help for "people problems" in the work place. I must emphasize that psychiatry essentially specializes in diagnosis and treatment of mental illness and may not be as competent or useful in areas of normal intrapsychic and interpersonal function as the other two. Being part

*Robert L. Meineker earned his M.D. degree at Albany Medical College. He is a Diplomate of the American Board of Psychiatry and Neurology in Psychiatry, and a Fellow of the American Psychiatric Association. Dr. Meineker is an Attending Psychiatrist at St. Vincent's Hospital in New York City and Assistant Attending Psychiatrist at Roosevelt Hospital. In addition to the private practice of psychiatry, specializing in psychotherapy, he has served as Chief of the Psychiatric Outpatient Department of St. Vincent's Hospital from 1955 to 1960. From 1960 to 1973 he was Psychiatric Consultant to the Continental Insurance Companies and is still active in occupational psychiatric consultation. Since 1973 Dr. Meineker has been Director of Psychiatric Ambulatory Services at St. Vincent's Hospital and Medical Center.

of medicine gives psychiatry advantages in management of certain kinds of problems but also creates certain drawbacks, i.e., stigma of mental illness, too often seeing process as illnesses with insufficient view of normal psychological and social dynamics. I shall try to confine myself to psychiatry and leave the other areas to those with more appropriate training and experience.

Psychiatry can be useful in preventing or remedying worker misfits in industry in two major ways:

1. Recognition of people at high risk for emotional or social disability, that is, case-finding by:

   a. Pre-employment screening
   b. Locating troubled people through the monitoring of absenteeism, accidents, and maladaptive behavior
   c. Assisting in medical department programs within companies

2. Therapeutic management of people with emotional problems

I plan to make only some general comments on the first category because I believe other sciences must be used simultaneously in these areas, which are not the primary province of psychiatry. Then, I shall illustrate how psychiatry proper can be useful in relieving what appears to be a misfit in industry by presenting actual cases on which I have consulted.

In the area of pre-employment screening, psychiatry can be useful, but there are many pitfalls. A psychiatrist can identify active emotional illness in job candidates and recommend against employment, but its occurrence is so rare that psychiatric screening for this is usually not economically practical. Acutely ill people (except manics) usually don't apply for jobs. If they do, it doesn't take an expert to recognize their illness. Furthermore, the psychiatrist is trained to pick out emotional problems rather than to evaluate how able a person is to work, so the psychiatrist may often create problems in hiring that work against the prospective employee. Too often he may be concerned with pathology which may not interfere with work. However, the psychiatrist, using interview techniques, can assess a total personality makeup, especially motivational potentials, in a way that many psychological tests cannot.

The problem for me as a pre-employment screener, however, was not so much in the area of assessing the prospective employee, as it was in understanding exactly what management wanted in the position. I often saw situations where management was threatened by psychiatric screening. Many qualities which I thought would be desirable in people for the job, were often rejected by management. In the end, management really wanted to select people who were very much in their own mold and image and who possibly would not give management much competition. As a result, psychiatry often is not particularly effective in pre-employment screening. As a sidelight, recent equal opportunity social trends tend to preclude this sort of investigation as discriminatory.

In pre-employment work I found that motivation was, for the most part, more important than ability in predicting success on the job. High motivation seemed to make the man with even modest skills perform better than the man who had great inherent ability, but low motivation. In this work the psychiatrist must beware that his function is not primarily to assess illness as in his ordinary work, but to look for personality traits which will spell out motivation, needs for individual gratification, and defense patterns which will promote better adjustment to certain work conditions.

In the area of finding the emotionally troubled people in industry the psychiatrist can be a valuable adjunct by joining with the medical department, first-line supervisors, and middle management in reviewing absenteeism, accidents, and incidents of maladaptive behavior. These behaviors frequently signal emotional problems in the work area which his clinical skills can spot, and then his group therapy skills can aid the review group in working together to devise remedies for each case.

Finally, availability of psychiatric consultation in the company medical department is very valuable, because so many emotional conflicts in the work place are presented as physical complaints to the medical department. It is important to see that these people are not overly studied by laboratory tests or medicated for physical illnesses which they really don't have. It is most important that the emotional conflict be identified so that the employee can develop better coping mechanisms.

Before turning to examples of psychiatric malfunctioning, I would like to make some comments about four terms that have been used in defining the theme of this conference on "Misfits In Industry." The terms are: over-educated, over-qualified, mistrained, under-employed.

Over-education is usually found in people who don't know what they want, are scared of life, and tend to be slated for failure. Formal education in itself, as an end, is actually worth little in being successful in life. Rather, what is needed more is a vigorous, self-reliant, interested, loving attitude. Many of the most successful people are actually self-made rather than formally educated.

As to being over-qualified for a job, I don't believe there is any such thing essentially. I find the term "over-qualified" being used most often by personnel managers as an excuse to get out of hiring someone. Too often personnel practices in our country result in under-qualified people being placed in jobs they can't handle. I admit, however, that there are situations where well-trained, bright people would become bored, but here again, if they needed the work badly enough their motivation would probably make them successful. For the most part, so-called over-qualified people should be, and are, perfectly able to decide when a job isn't right for them and they rarely need others to make such decisions.

When workers are mistrained this is most often the fault of management and educators who don't really understand what skills are necessary for particular jobs. Unfortunately, we have been going through an era when education and training are seen as prerequisites for a job, and actual on-the-job training has often been down-played, neglected, or done impractically. Actually, there is no substitute for learning on the job. Formal education courses often do not really supply the skills that are needed in the actual work place American youth and the Congress often act as though education is primarily an individual right because it will assure employment. Education actually is important for the development of the individual, but the skills he needs to work can usually best be learned on the job.

Finally when we investigate the under-employed, we should be aware that the incidence of personality disorder, psychosis, alcoholism, addiction, sexual dysfunction, and sociopathy is very high in this group. Actually, a rather large portion of the unemployed may be unemployable. The psychiatric problems contributing most to unemployment are among the most intractable to treatment. This fact seems to be admitted rarely, often even denied by psychiatrists. We can only hope that research will shed new light on these problems.

Now, I shall turn to the area where psychiatry is most useful in remedying employment problems, the management of people with emotional illness. I have chosen recent examples from my practice that include middle-age depression, alcoholism, manic-depressive illness, personality disorder, and paranoid psychosis.

The first illustration of psychiatry at work to alleviate misfits on the job, is a case of depression hiding alcoholism in a young woman whose basic personality structure is somewhat immature and passive-dependent.

M.D. was a 31-year-old single, white female employed as a sales representative for a large hotel. She sought psychiatric help on the advice of her sister, a nurse, because she was finding it hard to keep up on the job. She complained that she was falling apart and every little task seemed like a huge problem for her and upset her unduly. She felt depressed and often had to relieve emotional tension with a drink. Two weeks prior to consultation she had made a superficial cut on her wrist and it was this act that prompted her sister to refer her for psychiatric help.

The patient lived with her sister and another roommate. She admitted to occasional insomnia and fluctuating appetite with a tendency to overeat when depressed. She denied taking drugs or tranquilizers but admitted that she was frequently insecure and unhappy.

History revealed that the patient came from an upper-middle-class family.

Her father was a 69-year-old healthy man who ran an insurance agency. He was described by the patient as warm, outgoing, and overprotective. She thought he was great and claimed that she was closer to him than to her mother. Her mother had died suddenly at the age of 51 of a ruptured aneurysm in the brain. The patient stated that she was ambivalent about her mother whom she said was warm and good, but also a disciplinarian. It was this aspect of the mother that the patient resented. Her father often took her side against the mother. The mother and father were said to be close. The patient was the second of four children. Her sister, 36, married, with four children, was described as opinionated and strong. A sister, 25, who was single and a nurse, lived with the patient and was described as close, quiet, and deep. She seemed to imply to the patient that she thought the patient was weak and always took the easy way out. The youngest sister was 24, married two years, and expecting a baby. The patient's father had remarried after the mother's death and, at that time, the patient moved out of the house to live with her sister. There was no history of mental illness in the family.

The patient described her childhood as happy, although she was often scared and cried and suffered much separation anxiety when she started school. She claimed she had many friends but was terrified by the nun teachers. Her ambition was to grow up, marry, and have a family. She dated a lot in high school and had many friends. She became engaged to a Navy man and this seemed to be the climax of this period of development. They had gone together two years when the fiance broke the engagement saying he was not mature enough to marry (although he married within three years). The patient was heartbroken and this episode marked the onset of a gradual decline during her 20's. For a long time she felt rather depressed, as though her life were falling in. No other man could seem to replace her fiance and she became more afraid of being alone. She did not go to college but worked for a real estate company for three years and then a construction company for two years. Since then she has been in the hotel field.

After her engagement broke, she became friendly with a married man for four years. The affair culminated in sexual relations, a pregnancy, and an abortion even though she was a firm Catholic. She still pursues this rather hopeless relationship and it represents an example of her masochism. It was during this time that her mother died, which brought about even deeper feelings of depression than would be expected, and the patient felt more helpless. She saw herself as passive and insecure. She did not like herself and began to use alcohol more frequently. During the first interview she was unwilling to admit just what her drinking patterns were and how much she drank. The final big blow in her life was when her father remarried and she had to leave home to live with her sister, who always indicated disapproval of the patient's inability to face issues squarely.

From this first interview it was assumed that this patient had a personality disorder manifested by a good deal of dependency, which was first clearly illustrated by the separation anxiety from her mother when she started school, and her overly modest ambitions in life, even lack of ambition. She was totally unable to cope with an engagement she might have made work if she had reassured her fiance and played her cards differently. The mother's death and the father's alliance with another woman seemed to have smothered her ambition and led to increasing helplessness, failure on the job, depressive mood, drinking, and superficial wrist slashing. A diagnosis of reactive depression was made and psychotherapy advised.

The following week the patient reported that she felt calmer and relaxed but she obviously had great difficulty talking about herself in therapy. As the interview progressed she became increasingly paralyzed and I tried to be supportive and encouraging indicating that it was not unusual for people to be silent when they came face-to-face with their problems. I suggested that she keep notes about her feelings during the week. In the next session the patient had some notes and said that she thought a lot about why she had gone into therapy. She stated that she thought she did it for her family (not herself). During the week she couldn't sleep much and was awake for hours at night thinking. She stated that never before had she had a similar experience. On Friday she lost her job. She still blamed her disability more on external circumstances, suggesting that the department was phasing out, but she did not face her own failure to perform. Her sister taunted her about what she was going to do about a job and told her bluntly that she was lazy and didn't assume responsibility well. Apparently there had been considerable drinking and when the sister scolded her, the patient became angry. When I asked about the drinking she denied it.

I then asked her why she seemed to take the easy way out so often and wouldn't fight for what she wanted, suggesting that this might be one of the major problems that had to be worked on in therapy. After some thought, the patient suggested that possibly she expected her father to protect her and, as a matter of fact, he did. In the next session the patient claimed she felt very good. She had had a date and enjoyed it. However, she indicated that she was apprehensive about today's session. She had not been doing much in her life except nursing a friend who was just out of the hospital. She did not feel any sense of accomplishment in this but described it as confining and annoying. It is quite obvious that in this session the patient was unable to face her passivity and resistance.

This resistance, passivity, masochism, and depression culminated in a suicidal attempt in which the patient took many sedative pills while drinking and was brought to the emergency room of the hospital by her sister. I saw her the next day on the ward in the hospital where she was extremely tearful and admitted to heavy use of alcohol, much greater than she had admitted originally to me. Apparently she was in the habit of drinking episodically two or three days in a row every week or two. Her attitude was generally tearful, remorseful, but not deeply depressed. She seemed quite relieved, in a sense, to be in the hospital. Realizing that insight therapy would be impossible and dangerous as long as there was addiction to alcohol as an escape from facing problems, I referred her to the alcoholism unit. She obviously had to be sober before any further therapy could be undertaken.

Since then the patient has followed through with this and is attending A.A. and group therapy in the alcoholism outpatient unit. She looks much better and has found a job again. However, in all probability, she will still have to face her characterologic dependency, masochism, and depression in future psychotherapy. It is too soon to insist she do this. Premature pressure could precipitate drinking again.

This case illustrates how characterologic problems, alcoholism, and depression can interfere with job adjustment. Management of these problems, hopefully, will make it possible for this young woman's fourth decade of life to be much happier and to lead to some personal fulfillment.

The second example is a case of manic-depressive illness, presenting first with paranoid symptomatology and diagnosed as paranoid schizophrenia.

I first saw Mrs. S., a 37-year-old married woman in Feburary 1974. She worked overseas with her husband for a large chemical corporation. She had been referred for consultation by the medical department because of three periods of psychiatric illness in the last two years. Apparently, the first episode had been quite mild and consisted of paranoid ideation. This episode responded easily to psychotherapy. The second episode early in January 1973 was considerably more severe and characterized by frank paranoid delusions, restlessness, and insomnia. There was little weight loss and the patient denied depression. She was treated in Athens, Greece, with Thorazine, Stelazine, and Valium, and with electroshock. She made a good recovery, but in August 1973 there was a relapse characterized by euphoria, hyperactivity, and paranoid ideation again. This episode responded to Stelazine, Largactil (Thorazine) and Phenergan.

There was no history of mental illness in the family. She did not seem to have a history of previous depressions or periods of overactivity, which would point to a definite diagnosis of manic-depressive illness with paranoid features. She had always been an active, energetic woman who had a strong sense of dedication to her job and who kept a strong reign on herself emotionally. There were no depressions following the death of her father or her first husband or after the birth of her children. Generally she claimed to like dwelling in foreign countries with her husband. She was concerned about certain signs of approaching middle age, such as change in the texture of her skin and hair, the appearance of slight facial hirsutism and some loss of energy. She attributed all of these to the tranquilizer medications. While they may have contributed, they probably were not responsible for the total picture. The woman seemed devoted to her husband and job responsibilities and showed considerable anxiety about keeping everything in perfect operating order. She became impatient with people who had weaknesses and couldn't get jobs done, such as her husband's secretary. She made rigid, high demands on her own performance and showed almost an exaggerated need to hide any feelings of pressure or weakness on her part.

On mental status at that time the patient was vivacious, talkative, and showed no major pathology. It was evident that she had considerable insight into the fact that she did have paranoid delusions, and her attitude was cooperative and frank. There were no signs of depression or agitation and she was sleeping well. Her affect seemed essentially appropriate and of adequate depth. Many little anxieties about her adequacy were revealed. She was unhappy about the side effects of medication, which were really not too severe and which she had been tolerating.

Diagnostically it was my impression that the patient suffered from a paranoid state which may have been somewhat associated with her approaching middle age and involutional period. Actually, her menstrual period had stopped during some of her illness. I believed that the euphoria and overactivity, which had recently been evident, were probably more related to paranoid grandiosity than to any manic-like state. However, I could not rule out manic illness without further observations.

It was my prognosis that the patient might suffer further relapses in the future, but that the prognosis should be good so that she could continue her work in a foreign country. I suggested that if her mood became euphoric and overactive, prompt treatment with tranquilizers would be in order, and if, on the other hand, she became depressed and slowed down, anti-depressants were indicated.

Following this consultation the patient remained well until December 1974, when she developed another overactive euphoric episode but it did not manifest paranoid delusions. She was hospitalized and treated successfully with Phenothiazine tranquilizers. However, in June 1975, she had another episode of overactivity and was placed on Stelazine, Thorazine, Haldol, Akineton, and Valium. Her overactivity slowed down, but the patient began to feel greatly over-medicated. She looked dragged out, but there was no evidence of thinking disturbances and she related well in the interview. She disclaimed any feelings of depression saying that she actually had a good time during her current stay in the States. She had attended her sister's wedding and traveled a great deal. Currently, she was in her third week of vacation. She was sleeping long hours during the day, probably related to over-tranquilization.

In view of her repeated episodes of overactivity on the last two occasions without paranoid ideation, I felt that the diagnosis of manic-depressive illness bipolar type must be made. It was interesting that the episodes of over-activity occurred in the late spring and in December. Both of these times marked anniversary situations for the patient. Otherwise, there were no clear-ly identifiable precipitating circumstances for these changes in mood and activity. It is noteworthy, too, that no thinking disorder, except for increased rate of thinking, had occurred during these episodes. At that time I recom-mended Lithium therapy, but the patient was returning to Europe and there was no time to institute it.

In June 1976, I again saw the patient. Most recently she had been suffering from depression accompanied by some insomnia and feelings of great difficul-ty planning and getting even small tasks done. Her doctor in Athens had been treating her with Triptisol which is probably Elavil in this country. Her dosage had only been 30 to 40 mgs., per day for fear that it might push her into a high. Seeing that she was still depressed, I changed her medication to Tofranil 25 mgs., q.i.d., and after consultation with her husband, we decided to start her on prophylactic Lithium therapy. By June 11, we had her Lithi-um level already to 1.6 mgs. percent and the dosage was reduced. She com-plained of no toxic symptoms and finally we stabilized the blood level at about .8 mgs. percent. Her depression had improved rapidly, probably the re-sult of the Tofranil. She was sent back overseas with a supply of Tofranil for lows and Thorazine for highs, should they occur. However, since then the patient has reported that she has felt better than she has for a long time. There have been no undue mood swings. It is interesting to note that on Lithium the patient feels somewhat less energetic and calmer than she was ordinarily used to in her life, suggesting that probably she had always lived a little bit on the manic side.

This case is a good example of how psychiatry can help a person with serious emotional illness manage to maintain a good life adjustment and do her work. Unfortunately, time will not permit the presentation of the other cases. However, from these two, one can see examples of how psychiatric care made it possible for severely incapacitated people with work failure to resume productive lives.

DISCUSSION

Chaired by speaker Robert Meineker, M.D., the panel of psychiatrists included:

Stuart Keill, M.D., Chairman, Department of Psychiatry and Psychology, Nassau County Medical Center; Professor of Clinical Psychiatry, School of Medi-cine, Health Sciences Center, State University of New York at Stony Brook
Duncan R. MacMaster, M.D., private practice, Litchfield, Connecticut
Edward Malone, M.D., Clinical Director, South Oaks Hospital
Tadao Ogura, M.D., Staff Psychiatrist, South Oaks Hospital

Audience:

Women have increased enormously in our work force in the past few years, and many of these women have young children. What effect will this have on the children who, in turn, will grow up and join the work force?

Dr. MacMaster:

You don't reprimand a child two or three hours after he has done something. You've got to be there when it needs to be done. If you are going to have input regarding his behavior, you can't be absent. In general, it is my opinion that it is better to have a parent at home. But, from the opposite end of the spectrum, it is not so much the quantity of mothering but the quality of the mothering that counts. Actually, many times the child benefits from the mother being stimulated and happy and having herself more fulfilled because of her job role.

Again, as a generality, as long as you have a consistency and a pattern of behavior in your home that is pretty healthy, whether the mother is working or not working doesn't have too much to do with the outcome of the children, provided you have a consistent structure in which the child can grow up. That is more important than the fact of whether or not the mother is working outside the home.

Audience:

Possibly a father will be a better father if the mother is working.

Dr. MacMaster:

I don't think that whether the mother is working or not is going to determine whether or not a particular father is going to be a better parent.

Dr. Meineker:

Time and time again I've been disappointed in fathers in general because of their lack of involvement. Too often they feel that making the money and bringing the paycheck home is all they have to do. There is simply no doubt that the changing roles of women in our society will have effects on the family, on the children, but somehow I think socially we will be able to manage it.

Dr. Ogura:

Traditionally, Japanese women have been confined to the home, but after World War II the home underwent a tremendous transformation. Women became more active in society and also started actively pursuing their own interests for their own pleasure. These days many husbands have to leave their homes without eating breakfast because their wives don't get up. Also, many children come to school without their lunch because again, their mothers have stayed out too late and didn't get up.

Dr. Keill:

I think the fact that the children were allowed to go to school without their lunches is not so much a reflection of the fact that the mother is working, but shows that the sense of responsibility of the mother and the father to each other and to the children is such that they both are willing to abdicate their responsibility to the family unit.

Of course, there is an infinite variety of potential clinical problems when parents are absent from the home. However, the healthy absence of a mother who wishes to fulfill herself and work creatively could have a beneficial effect. Someone talked about the advantages of having a greater exposure of the children with the father. If the father is an individual who is unemployed because of his own personality difficulties, further exposure might be damaging to the child. Similarly, exposure to an unhappy mother who is constantly railing against her situation would also be bad for the child. The future mental health of the present younger generation may be affected, but I don't think it will be changed materially. The relative stability of two parents in relation to their children is going to have the ultimate effect on them.

Dr. Meineker:

I'd like us to move on to a discussion of pre-employment screening.

Dr. Keill:

As has been said, it is very difficult at times for a psychiatrist to predict success for an individual in an organization without being very clear on what the organization wants from an individual. Some years ago I had a similar but, in a way, simpler job than Dr. Meineker's job with the insurance company. I was involved in some preliminary screening of new Marine recruits who had recently arrived at Parris Island. I say simpler because, in the first place, the job description of a Marine recruit is much more clearly demarcated than one for an insurance agent. The ways that Marine recruits could get in trouble was also much clearer. There was much isolation from everything outside the boot camp at Parris Island, so there was less chance for anti-therapeutic interferences from the outside world.

My predecessor at Parris Island had set up a system to evaluate performance by the professional staff which gave us a minute and a half to interview each recruit. In that period we had to make a prediction as to how well the recruit would perform in the next 2 weeks, in the next 12 weeks, and in the next two years in the Marine Corps stateside and, if necessary, on the battlefield. You had to write it down during the minute and a half that you were interviewing the recruit.

This was one of the most valuable experiences of my life because I was forced to make decisions and then stand by them when they were checked on two weeks later, 12 weeks later, and so on. One of the reasons my job was simpler was because all of these young men had had rather traumatic experiences for the three or four days before the interview. They had left home, often for the first time, and were separated from their family and kind. Many of the them were not secure anyway; they were only 17 or 18 years old. They had been brought in the middle of the night to a very strange part of the country. Parris Island with its swamps and vines was a depressing sight.

They were then immediately separated from all of their belongings, including their jewelry and their hair and their clothes, and made to walk around and get a variety of injections and physicals. They were constantly being yelled at, I might add. Then, just prior to seeing the psychiatrist, they were given two psychological tests, and then they were thrust, physically almost, into this room for their minute and a half session with the psychiatrist. The recruits, usually trembling, held tests in their hands which had results you could analyze while you were asking them provocative questions.

When I did get around shortly thereafter to taking some formal psychiatric training I was up on some of my colleagues because I was used to making sudden decisions, quick decisions clinically which were pointed at when they were wrong. It was a valuable experience and we were able to predict the kinds of difficulties that these recruits would get into and at what stage.

The problem of evaluation in industry is a pretty complicated one and I think in many ways differs from situations like the Army or the Peace Corps where the job has legal aspects to it and is quite uniform.

One of the speakers said that companies now have to be socially responsible to a certain extent and that, while it would be a marvelous idea to pre-select everyone and hire only the best in order to have a great working force, actually this is not possible or really very desirable at all; in many ways you have to experiment a little bit. Many companies use various types of psychological tests and some of them are quite good. But we know that young people around 19 and 20 are very apt to be unstable on the job. They tend to have frequent absences and may have crises in their lives. They are not used to being devoted to the "good old firm" so they take certain liberties which the boss doesn't like and they may run into little hassles.

Pre-employment screening from a psychiatric standpoint sounds very good but, in many ways, the psychiatrist should be quite cautious about making sweeping decisions concerning anybody's career or job opportunities; in many ways you have to be prepared to help people to work no matter how unfit they are for it.

Audience:

Many people have emotional problems but yet, given the chance, they function on a certain job.

Dr. Meineker:

That is true. A lot of pretty sick people can do good jobs at times.

Audience:

What we have been talking about so far is how to keep misfits out. When misfits are in, employees who need help in coping with some of their problems, we need supportive systems that can be used by staff to deal with them.

Dr. Malone:

Here's a case in point. Grumman Aircraft has, for some time, been sending experts to Iran to help repair various aircraft there. These men went over for at least two years, and the enticement was that the substantial salaries would be tax-free. However, this has led to a number of problems because the housing and the schooling in Iran are not very good, and consequently, many of these men were going to be separated from their families. They were in a position of being torn between two wishes, the wish to make money and the wish to be with their families. This led to some steady employment on our part in counseling these people. This is one example of people doing very well in situations and then, because of some change, all of a sudden they run into emotional problems. It has been my experience that Grumman handles these cases very well because they have a medical department and they are aware of the resources in the community and they refer to them with a good deal of success.

Dr. Ogura:

In every society, when we have somebody who doesn't fit the system we tend to exclude them in one way or another, whether they are over-qualified or under-qualified.

As psychiatrists, we have to be more concerned about those people who temporarily become misfits due to some mental illness. These people tend to be pushed out of the system and labeled as "nuts." However, they could resume their full capacity in due time if the system would allow them to stay in a little longer.

I had a patient who had a nervous breakdown which was not related to his employment. After he went back to work, he stayed on borderline for about three months. He became quite depressed most of the time and couldn't feel energetic enough to function to his satisfaction. Fortunately, in this particular case, his colleagues gave him tremendous support, physically as well as emotionally.

Because of this support he survived the crisis and now is in such good shape that he is hoping to get a promotion. But if he hadn't had this support, probably he would have been fired by now. Actually, he had once been called up to the medical department and had been told that he might be let go.

Dr. Keill:

I personally question the term over-qualified as a meaningful clinical one. The over-qualified person, if he has a basically satisfactory relationship with the significant parts of his world, can deal with his job in one or two ways. He can either move to a position which is more appropriate to his background, or, as long as the job frustration continues, he can get this satisfaction out of some other aspect of his life. There is a problem I think, if his job becomes the battleground of his clinical sense of equality; then his employer, his co-workers, and those of us in mental health have a responsibility to help out.

Dr. Meineker mentioned at one point that we psychiatrists have to be careful to limit ourselves to what we are good at, the diagnosis and treatment of disabilities. For a long time, especially in the 50's, and early 60's, I think some of us tended to feel that the psychiatrist had the answers to all the problems in the world and now we are beginning to limit ourselves, many of us, to diagnosis and treatment.

Audience:

Mental health professionals, particularly psychiatrists, focus on illness and diagnosis. I'd like to hear more about prevention and treatment.

Dr. MacMaster:

I think that treatment always begins with prevention. If one is interested in treatment, one has to be interested in prevention and maybe this is what this conference is all about. From my point of view, one of the things that has interested me very much is the business of the borderline cases. The borderline psychotic often is, on paper, over-qualified but really isn't over-qualified at all because he can't do anything; at least he can't do anything very well. What I have found is that such a person gets into an employment situation where he manages to work himself up to a certain position where he is overloaded. Much like a hyperactive child, he gets overloaded and then you have short-circuiting and the person stops functioning.

A psychiatrist functions well, I think, in industry when these people can be identified, not marked in terms of people becoming prejudiced against them or making them scapegoats, which I have also seen, but rather marked in a sense that there is something wrong when a person keeps going up to a certain point and then breaks down.

I have a particular case in mind concerning a man, a Phi Beta Kappa, who was the guidance director for a very large public high school. He kept advancing and made the school system work a little differently. After about seven years he had a real psychotic break and went into the hospital. He went through this for a long period of time, that is, in and out of hospitals over a 10-year period. At one point he came under my care and he told me that his 14-year-old daughter had concluded that maybe he would be much better off somewhere else or doing something else. This option had never occurred to anybody because this man had an outstanding intellect. But he was emotionally labile and very immature, and obviously could become psychotic in a work situation where he took on the kind of responsibility where he was allowed to roam loose in a rather abstract area of people, lots of people, lots of problems, and all kinds of conflict.

To make a long story short, I encouraged him and helped him to get a job, an ordinary everyday job. It was a low-paying, mundane, workaday job and I told him if he wanted to pursue it, fine. He could bring some of his craziness to me; we could deal with it and keep him functioning. Very gradually this man began to enjoy his job. He did plating, which involved a great deal of tactile, sensory work. He never had another psychotic break from that time to this, which is about 10 years. It is the sort of case you think about in terms of what can you do. Some times if the pressure pulse is taken, the psychiatrist can deduce a great deal.

Dr. Meineker:

Certainly, psychiatrists can promote prevention in the occupational area, as we have agreed, by counseling. We know that certain types of behavior suggest that an employee is in trouble, such as staying home, coming in late, getting into arguments, having accidents, and drinking on the job. So you should look at the accident-prone employee, the employee who has a pattern of absenteeism, or the employee with a lot of physical complaints who keeps coming to see the nurse or doctor. These are the employees who might very well have some emotional problems.

A good way to help these people is to get together with others who are involved with the troubled employee, a first-line supervisor, somebody from personnel, somebody from the medical department, the psychiatrist, a counselor. Such a meeting produces a tremendous amount of information. It often was too apparent that some of the problems were caused by lack of communication between various departments, and by lack of communication between management and the union. It is a marvelous way to nail down problems but it takes quite a bit of skill.

Audience:

There are social, cultural, and political pressures on the worker which may have nothing to do with the job itself. His inability to adjust himself to these environmental pressures may be causing him to become an emotionally ill misfit.

Dr. Meineker:

In the early days, when I first went into occupational psychiatry, it was part of the theory that most of the real problems were the result of emotional conflicts outside of the workplace. I think there is a great deal in that, although there certainly are some very real problems in the work place too.

Recently a middle-aged woman was referred to me because she had shaking hands. She was a 46-year-old married woman who was an open, friendly type. She was compliant in her responses and always tried to please. I learned that she came to work on the subway every morning. Recently the number of subway cars in Manhattan has been cut in half; it may conserve power to run only half as many cars on the train, but it certainly upsets people a good deal. By the time they get into work in the morning, after being pushed, shoved, and jostled around, they often don't want to even say good morning to their fellow workers. This woman was working with about eight other people who came in grimly in the morning and sat down at their desks and went to work and didn't smile, didn't pass the time of day. She became increasingly nervous on the job and began to wonder, in a paranoid way, whether it was something she was doing. Did she smell, so to speak, or what was wrong with her? She began to shake and she saw the doctor who suggested she see the psychiatrist. We discussed all the aspects of coming to work in the morning and talked about the social problems of the city. As a psychiatrist I was concerned with her dependency and her need for reassurance, but I used quite simple external means, almost rationalizing her problem for her. She was reassured and went back to work with very little trouble.

So, a lot of psychiatric practice in the occupational area has to be adapted to the setting. Long-term therapy isn't indicated. You can accomplish a great deal by just helping the individual to cope with immediate problems.

Dr. Malone:

In the situations described here there is an element of change, either social, economical, or political. Some people have enough ego strength to handle changes in their life situation. Others need help during periods of change. Any kind of change, promotion, movement, political changes, changes in subway systems, and so forth, can cause people to become misfits.

Audience:

Should mental health people actually be involved in social and political changes to help the misfit?

Dr. Meineker:

When I was younger, I had a lot more zeal. I now have retreated to a position where I see that my main power comes from people coming to me for help rather than my going out and saying, you've got such-and-such kind of trouble.

Dr. Malone:

I think our track record is very bad when we become assertive. I believe we should still maintain a relatively passive style.

Dr. Keill:

I agree. I had a friend who was a brilliant individual who happened to go into psychiatry. He somehow was a misfit in psychiatry because, as it turned out, he felt he should change his career. He became a director of an important community program in a large New York City hospital. He used to talk to us, his colleagues, about how he discussed things with the inner-city residents of the community near the hospital. He would say to them, "You know what you really need, you need power. You are not mentally ill, you have to have power and until you have power, and jobs, and money, you will be depressed all the time, and I will know when you have finally become well, when you seize the power and have me fired." He used to tell us this with great delight. Well, he actually was fired, and the community took over the hospital. When patients started to die, they threw the community out and started to rebuild the hospital.

There was a great movement in the 50's and 60's when many rather grandiose colleagues really thought they had a lot of answers to the problems of society and the problems of the world. They thought that if a psychiatrist sat at the United Nations we would have world peace, and if a psychiatrist became president of the United States, then everything would be all right. Fortunately for us, they didn't manage to get into these positions. I believe that we, and the people we are trying to help, are better off if we stick to the kinds of things that we have been trained to do and at least that we are good at.

Audience:

Shouldn't we give some consideration to where so-called misfits come from? They are miseducated and they become misfits. They are mistrained and they become misfits. Are any of you making any effort to give input to your local school systems and training institutions?

Dr. Meineker:

I'd like someone in the audience to comment about what education ought to be.

Audience:

We have an employee, in her late 40's, with a fourth-grade education, who had worked at various factory jobs before she came to us as a food service worker. We found that she couldn't read the menu or the tray cards, and went over lessons with her. She finally was able to read at a fourth-grade time to have a young woman working for us part-time who was majoring in teaching reading to educationally handicapped people. She began an educational program and the woman's sister supported this program, tutored her and went over lessons with her. She finally was able to read at a fourth-grade level. We were quite proud of this woman's achievement and she was promoted to the next level.

Now, after five years, she is dissatisfied because she cannot be promoted higher. Every time she tries to be promoted to a journeyman-level worker, a job that requires extensive reading, she gets rejected. Nobody has had the courage to sit down with this woman and tell her that, because of her reading ability, she can never go beyond her present level. She thinks she has not been selected because of her nationality and various other reasons, and she feels that the supervisors are against her. She is becoming paranoid about her lack of selection. Here is a case where education fostered a misfit.

Audience:

In my own experience, a person who is a misfit in industry is a misfit, period. I think that number one, we must change our educational systems so that teachers from kindergarten up learn to have an awareness of each individual child, each individual child's family background. They must have a good, deep knowledge of psychology and then the personal interest and the capacity to make each child feel worthwhile and important. Of course, there is no such thing as a perfect answer for every problem.

Dr. Keill:

Yes, I think that is about it. There are no simple answers. But we can't sit back and say we'll have to wait until the educational system is changed.

I'd like to comment further on the woman who is unhappy because she is not being promoted. Although she was placed in a job for which she was not suited, she did rather well because of some major efforts by people who were concerned for her. However, she is now getting to the point where she seems to have a clinically definable illness. She is becoming paranoid, she feels discriminated against, she feels persecuted. Now most of us would agree that in almost any case of paranoia there is always an element of truth, and I think in this case you confirmed that there was an element of truth. You yourself said you and others were causing her harm because you were reluctant to tell her the real reason why she was not being promoted. Now this is embarrassing and difficult for anybody to say. It is like saying, "You should bathe more often, you know, you smell bad," or, "You haven't been educated enough." But, with some sensitivity and some clinical knowledge, there are ways of dealing with this problem. You may not need a psychiatrist but I think that you, or one of your colleagues, with some assistance from some fundamental people, should sit down with this woman and say, "This is the real problem; let's have it out in the open, let's talk about it, and maybe you can do something about it." Whether you can change her abilities or not, you can at least increase the chances that she won't be a misfit in that job.

Dr. Ogura:

Misfits are misfits no matter what kind of job or what kind of situation they may be in. Consistent misfits seem to be born losers. But there are other kinds of misfits. They are transitional misfits in a situation associated with change, promotion, family conflict, transfer, and so forth. I think there has to be some distinction between these two groups. Not all misfits are born losers; some misfits are transitional or temporary misfits. When it comes to born losers, I used to maintain a negativistic view that there are people who appear to be born losers. Freud wrote a paper on the "failure syndrome" in which he described people who try hard to almost purposefully fail. Recently, a new type of therapy developed to deal with these people has been quite successful. This therapy can change born losers to successful people.

Dr. Meineker:

Dr. MacMaster, would you like to comment about differences between education to develop the individual and education for technical purposes?

Dr. MacMaster:

As an industrial consultant I have been involved with the education of management and of people who are associated with personnel, people who have something to say about who is going to be trained to do what and under what circumstances.

In terms of vocational rehabilitation I am constantly meeting people who are doing things that they shouldn't be doing, that is, work that is not appropriate. Unfortunately, many of these people try to beat the system because they are not motivated to do something for themselves, whether in a techni-cal or general education sense. They say, you do something for me, do some-thing to me. You feel like a man winding up the back of a robot to get them to run so that they will start work efficiently and perform a function. It is very disappointing; it is a terrible waste of money. So, what I have done is to find key people who work within the system and I have tried to get them to evaluate people more closely and not try to merely satisfy certain quotas.

Audience:

I would like to respond to the statement that school teachers should be well trained in psychology in the interest of their pupils. I know that, as a psychiatrist, I am continually taking refresher courses and reading journals, but I feel awfully inadequate at times because it is so difficult to keep up with the tremendous strides that are being made. It seems to me that if we were to do this with our school teachers, we'd have very fine psychologists, but I wonder how long they'd be teachers?

Audience:

I'd like to make a positive statement. The educational system is making an effort to sensitize the young boy and girl to vocational opportunities, and to values that they might expect from various vocations. This goes on through elementary school into high school and on to the college level. Professors in the different disciplines constantly receive literature to present to their stu-dents concerning job opportunities that arise in that particular discipline. That is an educational effort in the right direction, helping people to have a more realistic look into the world of work.

Dr. Meineker:

That certainly is a factor in motivation, and we come back to that again and again. Motivation makes all the difference in the world. How about the problem of integrating back into the work place people who have had serious emotional illnesses? If a person has been in a mental hospital and comes back to work he often finds that he has caused gossip for a number of weeks. It's a difficult work situation to re-enter.

Audience:

As you know, we have an alcoholism program here at South Oaks Hospi-tal, and we spend a good bit of time preparing the person for return to his job. We also spend several weeks with the family members to prepare them. About two weeks before the patient is ready for discharge, we work with the company and with the supervisor so they understand the problem. This facili-tates the matter a little bit, but there is a problem, no question about it.

Dr. Ogura:

In 1973, a large study was done at Moseley Hospital in London to investigate why a person who has gone through psychiatric services doesn't seem to come up to his or her previous functional level. Regardless of the diagnosis, whether it is an acute nervous breakdown or manic-depressive illness, or a simple depression, if a person has required a hospitalization in a psychiatric unit, after he leaves, he doesn't seem to function as he should.

In an effort to deal with this phenomenon, they figured that a gradual transition into society would be the answer. So they created sheltered workshops and halfway houses to train them to gradually go back into society. It didn't work. Then they figured, well, maybe more intensive aftercare would work. Instead of once a week, let's see them even five times a week. By giving them more support, they will be able to adapt themselves into the society much better. Again, it didn't work.

So finally they came to a conclusion: why don't we ask patients what's the matter with them? So they interviewed a large number of people and their families and found one common denominator, their negative view of themselves. In many cases, after having gone through mental illnesses, their self-image was shattered. They are now ex-mental cases. People around them will also see these individuals as ex-mental patients. As a result, these ex-patients feel a peculiar apprehension that other people might be looking down on them or talking about their mental illness. In addition, their families also fall into the same pitfall.

After these factors were found, they started intensive counseling with the patients as well as their families throughout this transitional period. As a result, many patients went back to previous functional levels.

Dr. Keill:

I would like to go back to something that Dr. MacMaster said about the importance of prevention. We learned in World War II and in the Korean War about the advantages of shortening the time period of patients with psychiatric disabilities so they were not removed too long from the major course of their life's activities.

This knowledge pointed up the advantage of having confidential facilities in local areas where early detection of difficulties can be made through good liaison between the community facilities and industry, for example. This type of early detection could rule out the need for a person to go to the hospital in the first place. Also, this type of intervention would prevent deterioration that causes a severe disruption in relations between the patient and his fellow employees. This, I think, is one of the real responsibilities of a partnership between the mental health professionals and management.

CHAPTER 3

Management Looks at the Mis-Employed

DANIEL E. KNOWLES*

In the classical sense of examining, dissecting, and analyzing any topic is the initial requirement of defining our terms. Our misfits in industry come in many forms, not only the commonly thought of types such as, our large under-employed population who have been over-trained or mistrained, and our unemployed, young, middle-aged and older workers, our minorities and women, but also our less thought of types such as, our over-achievers, our unmotivated, frustrated, angry, lethargic, apathetic, misunderstood, alcoholic, emotionally disturbed workforce.

In a sense, all of us to a greater or lesser degree, sooner or later, eventually fall prey to the title of "misfit." Between alcoholism, mental/emotional problems, cancer, cardiovascular and sundry medical, political, personal, and interpersonal relationship problems, there is no way we can get out of life alive. We eventually all fall victim. Let's be realistic, not prophets of doom

---

*Daniel Knowles is Director of Personnel for the Grumman Aerospace Corporation, a firm employing over 21,000 workers. He majored in psychology and received his Master's degree at Hofstra University. Mr. Knowles' background in personnel relations is extensive and includes two years with the U.S. Army as a personnel psychologist. He is on the faculty of the New York Institute of Technology where he teaches courses on personnel management, collective bargaining, and labor relations. He has lectured for the American Management Association, and is currently writing a book on affirmative action for the middle-aged and older worker.

and gloom; there is no panacea for curing all the ills of all the misfits. Today our society with all its resources, good intentions, energy, altruism, and love, is primarily in the business of applying Band-Aids to the walking wounded. Again, this is not a defeatist, disheartened, fatalistic, give-up attitude, but rather an opinion of where we are today, not where we should be tomorrow.

With the myriad of problems of over-, under-, and miseducated people, with medical, personal, work, and nonwork related problems, is it any wonder that some surveys have indicated as high as 80 percent of our workforce population is engaged in occupations that they deem to be unsatisfactory? Eighty percent of our people would prefer to be doing something other than what they are doing. Eighty percent of us, for one reason or another, have not achieved the level of self-actualization where we ourselves feel the work we're doing is important in itself, work in which we do not perceive the possibility of achievement, growth, recognition or even potential.

Let's trace how we become misfits as influenced by a number of factors such as, our own personal psychological development, the influences of society, the educational system with emphasis on the guidance counselors, and finally that pragmatic people-eater, big business.

At a very early age, we learn that rewards and punishments are geared to our overt behavior rather than to how we feel inside. As a little 3-year-old boy who cries in the dark, we learn, when reproached by our father who, in effect, says, "Big boys don't cry in the dark," that approval is won by refraining from crying, not by conquering the fear. From this time on, we begin to develop what the late Dr. Chappel, Chairman of the Psychology Department at Hofstra University, called the "private eye." It's in this "private eye" that we keep hidden all our fears, idiosyncrasies, and quirks of internal behavior. Added to this are the experiences of suffering tension, stress, grief, pain, fear, anxiety, and frustration. Sure, some of these sufferings can be expressed in compensating feelings of love and affection, faith, integrity, sense of competence, and altruistic attitudes in which our adaptive capacities are improved, but also we can express these sufferings in decompensating feelings such as bitterness, suspicion, hostility, and self-centeredness, resulting in drives for power and competitiveness. The manifestations of these sufferings can result in our adaptive capacity remaining intact. We can also use escape devices such as hard work, alcohol, drugs, "hate group" membership. We can also acquire physical symptoms, and neuroses, such as depression. We can even act out our feelings. These psychological feelings and experiences of our first 20 years or so become the breeding ground of our future success in industry and our personal lives, or they become the causes of the label "misfit" in our personal or business life, or both.

Although it is difficult to isolate each of the contributing factors to the birth of a misfit, suffice it to say each of us bears a major responsibility in our own destiny, be it as a "misfit" or a "good fit" in our occupational life, as well as our personal life. Too often we look for excuses outside ourselves to blame for our failures. It becomes easy to develop a kind of non-psychotic paranoia and blame our role of misfit on being black, or female, or handicapped, or middle aged, or Irish, or Jewish. I never met a misfit who wasn't partially responsible for his own condition. It's a cop-out to blame all our problems on our parents, our schools, our religions, our educational institutions, and our businesses. Each of us has a responsibility for our own fortunes and futures. Lord knows that the other elements of society contribute to the misfits of this world by sins of commission as well as omission, by misdirection and miscommunication, but the old adage remains, "God helps those who help themselves." Another important psychological component in avoiding the role of misfit lies in another adage, "Know thyself." Many maladjusted individuals in the industrial setting are the result of an unrealistic evaluation of their own worth. There should be a reasonable relationship between ego and talent. It is healthy to think we are slightly better than we actually are, but the misfit oftentimes is the individual who perceives his talents to be light years away from his real abilities. Conversely, it is not psychologically healthy to undersell or understate you abilities either.

Now, let's examine our educational system today. Fact: Of 10 students today in the United States, two receive occupational training in high school; seven go beyond high school; four receive Bachelor degrees. Assuming two of the four who graduated from college are prepared for some sort of work, which is a very generous assumption indeed, then six of every 10 students today are not prepared for any specific occupation and the other four presumably are equipped to enter the workforce with nothing to offer other than raw potential.

Approximately a year ago, I gave a talk to a group of college registrars and high school guidance counselors. The title of the talk was "The End of the Liberal Arts Era." The speech was met with a certain degree of hostility on the part of some of the audience. It was, essentially, a rejection of reality. Twenty-five years ago when there was a smaller college graduate population, companies were more likely to be willing to accept the liberal arts graduate. Today in the era of advanced technology, the demand for technologically trained personnel has increased dramatically. This demand has increased not only for the scientifically trained, but also the business trained individual. And yet, the college system in this country is still, to a large degree, hanging on to the traditional system of educating its students for disillusionment, frustration, and ego deflation, by not preparing them for an occupational role in society. This is not a crusade against the humanities, but rather a cry for a more pragmatic approach to education; for a system that prepares the student for, not only an aesthetic life, but for a life of meaningful work. It is a fact of life for most of us, excluding a small group of the indulgent rich, that we must earn a living. While it is true that many young people can change their career goals and course of study, it is equally true that they must be educated, if not trained, to enter the pragmatic institution of work.

Wherein lies the fault in the educational system? Probably in at least three areas:

1. *Curriculum.* Over-emphasis in the field of general academic subjects, with little or no concern for the work world in which a student will eventually spend five days a week, for 50 weeks a year for 40-plus years.

2. *Orientation/Awareness Programs.* An abyssmal lack of programs to educate the student in the nature of work: career information in terms of types of jobs, prerequisites for attaining those professions, forecasts of the availability of jobs, typical remuneration for various careers, and other related information.

3. *Guidance Counselors.* Too often the guidance counselors in high schools are so preoccupied with the college-bound that little or no care is given to the work-bound. There is no quicker way to swell the ranks of the industrial misfits than to turn loose six of every ten graduates into the job market without an education in the nature of work; without the knowledge or training to compete for available jobs; without a direction towards fields which the students' mostly unexplored interests or aptitudes would suggest. The lack of education and knowledge of the typical guidance counselor in the world of work is a significant contribution to the continuing influx of misfits into the society of work. Given the opportunity, I would change the requirements for certification as a guidance counselor to make mandatory an apprenticeship in industry or business.

The guidance counselor is probably the second biggest contributor to the misfit in business today, right after the misfit himself. The work-bound probably, if they are fortunate, get more valuable information and guidance from the shop teachers and BOCES than they do from the guidance counselors.

Until such time as those in the educational system become better educated and trained in the world of work, or rather the understanding of the nature of work, we can expect to annually swell the ranks of potential misfits. It is a tribute to the young people themselves that many of them adapt to work considering the preparation they received.

Too often the Federal government, for self-serving purposes, has designed a number of programs, self administered, in the interest of retraining obsolete workers, the chronically unemployed. Again, too often those responsible for these programs are ill-equipped to train the misfit. Too often, people are trained for jobs for which no openings are available. After all, there are just so many beauticians needed in a given area. Too often the government perpetuates a fertile ground for the misfit by making welfare benefits more attractive monetarily than work. Even Congress has had to change legislation so that industry advisors are required when training programs run by the government are established. Perhaps government would be better advised to invest its money in programs run by industry to at least get a product or technology in return for its money, as well as employed workers. The government should understand that a misfit in industry is better than a misfit who is unemployed or on welfare.

The major factors predisposing an individual to becoming a misfit or a well-adjusted person at this point, are the life experiences of the individual, primarily psychological in nature; the educational process; and, to a lesser degree, the influence of government and society in general.

Given the previous factors, industry faces the integration of the needs of its employees, adjusted as well as maladjusted, with the needs of the organization. The purpose of the organization traditionally has been to return a profit to its stockholders. In recent years, however, business has perceived subsidiary purposes or goals. In addition to the profit motive, companies today recognize a social responsibility as well as the beginning of an awareness for responsibility for the quality of life of its employees. Pressures from society, government, and the employees themselves have resulted in a transition from the approach of first viewing the employee as a commodity, second, to one of paternalism and, more recently, to a more behavioral approach. A more educated employee today is demanding a more challenging work environment. Although the pressure is not as evident in today's recession, it is merely a temporary hiatus pending the return to a more prosperous economy in which the demand for qualified personnel will exceed the supply.

But, before further examining the demands of the present workforce, let's look at the various categories, causes, and conditions of the present misfits in industry today:

1. Under-educated employees—the employment of individuals in repetitive, unskilled, monotonous, highly methodized jobs. The result: boredom, frustration, discontent, and turnover.

2. Miseducated and over-educated employees—highly intelligent individuals being placed in jobs lacking challenge. The result: frustration.

3. Alcoholic, mentally ill, or emotionally disturbed employees. Alcoholics alone cost industry in excess of two billion dollars a year.

4. Frustrated employees who become misfits for the following reasons:
   —Lack of rapport between the employee and his boss, resulting in a breakdown in the interpersonal relationship.
   —Lack of visibility in the internal system and policies of the company, resulting in the perception of jobs being dead-ended.
   —Poor job design, resulting from over-methodization of job functions.

—Lack of opportunities for advancement as a function of the economic environment of the company.

—Lack of training within the organization. Employees who are unsure of what is expected and have to perform job functions become employees with poor morale and poor performance records, and who are hazards when it comes to safety procedures.

—Poor hygienic factors such as low wages, fringes, working conditions, and company and personnel policies.

—Lack of job security.

The list of ways and means of creating misfits is almost inexhaustible. In summary, however, the two broad categories of misfits are those that are already misfits when they enter the job market and those who become misfits as a result of the organizational systems of industry.

In addressing the first category, industry can contribute to the solution only in a minor degree and that is by a concerted effort to keep the communication channels open between educational and government agencies. In particular, industry must continue to urge educators to rethink the educational process. Educators must understand that the educational process, in addition to providing the student with a general understanding of his total environment, must also prepare the student, both psychologically and practically, for the world of work. Students, upon the completion of their education, must be prepared, with at least the minimum qualifications, for a skill or profession; otherwise the educational system has failed the individual in terms of the real world expectations of industry. Now, let's address what industry is doing and, more importantly, what industry is not doing in its interaction with the real or potential misfit.

Training is one of industry's great investments in lessening the impact of the misfit in the organization. From the day the employee starts work and attends an orientation or induction session, the company assumes the responsibility for the development of that person as a human resource for the dual goals of increasing the motivation and satisfaction of the employee's work goals, as well as attaining company goals.

Typical types of training techniques are vestibule on-the-job training, special courses, and apprenticeships, whereby employees are trained in the skills, systems, management, and human relations areas. The purpose of such training is to increase morale, reduce accidents and labor turnover, and increase productivity and quality of the job task. Various types of communications seminars help keep employees informed; often the Hawthorne effect of paying attention to people will aid in the integration of the individual into a more harmonious and better-adjusted role within the organization.

Analogous to inhouse training courses, both during and after working hours, is the offering of tuition refund program to employees. This provides the means for motivated employees, through work-related courses in colleges and universities, to reject the role of possible misfit by preparing for meaningful work within the organization. Sensitizing supervisory personnel through first-line, middle-management, and senior-management development programs, tends to lessen the impact of a disgruntled workforce by sharpening management's skills in establishing good working relationships between the supervisor and the employee. If one were to summarize the causes of misfits in industry, it could be attributed to two major conditions; first, to under-challenging or under-employing personnel and, second, to the lack of wholesome working relationships between employee and supervisors.

In the recent exit interviewing of a group of degreed business people, the following reasons for termination were cited: 18 terminating employees stated it was for lack of opportunity to advance; 15 said their talents were not being fully utilized; 12 stated that there was a lack of interest by supervision in subordinates; and, 5 were dissatisfied with wages.

The personnel development function, which is closely allied to the training function, serves a variety of purposes, such as monitoring the performance appraisal system to ensure that mangement is providing a periodic evaluation of an employee's performance, delineating the development needs of the employee as well as designing a development plan to satisfy those needs. In addition, providing some visibility to the employee as to his prospects for future advancement can reduce anxiety in the employee.

Career counseling by both supervisors and the personnel department is an essential technique for providing information, such as career paths, short- and long-range opportunities, and prerequisites for attaining those goals.

Posting of nonsupervisory and supervisory jobs is another technique important to the goal of providing visibility to the employee. Too often an employee's career is not planned through personnel systems but rather is allowed to meander along in a haphazard manner. Computerized systems cataloguing career information profiles or skills-inventory systems are becoming more popular in industry today as a means of providing management with summary and selective information.

Employee relations within the personnel function are taking on increased responsibility for the resolution of employee conflicts and problems today. Although most companies' policies state that they will be concerned only with work-related problems, in practice it only is a matter of time until personal problems are reflected on the job. That is why it is not uncommon within the personnel function to see programs to help the alcoholic, to help mentally and emotionally disturbed employees and, more recently, to help those with drug-related problems. Counseling concerning fiscal irresponsibility, incompatibility with supervision, and numerous other conflict situations commonly viewed as grievances, are concerns of the company whose interest is in the integration of employee and employer goals. This integration function is in actuality a function of motivation, an often confusing and little understood subject.

Also important are maintenance functions, such as employee service activities (hobby clubs, sports activities), services of the medical department, safety department activities, and cafeterias, which are provided by the company as a means of maintaining an employee who is already motivated or integrated.

Hygienic functions such as fair and equitable wages, fringe benefits, personnel policies, and good working conditions, are also important considerations in reducing the dissatisfaction of employees.

The above-stated functions merely scratch the surface in relation to industry's attempt to reduce the impact and numbers of misfits in the company today. The most important factor is the growing awareness on the part of the company to meet the individual requirements of a younger, better-educated, sophisticated, restless, dissatisfied employee who has accepted affluence as a part of his heritage, who is less likely to be affected by the depression syndrome and who may not consider the Protestant work ethic as something necessarily good.

For all the progress made by companies in recent years in responding to the needs of people, we still find ourselves shoveling sand against the tide.

Other vistas await industry in the future. In considering the theory of Abraham Maslow's hierarchy of needs, it is evident that man is striving for self-actualization, where he will feel that his work is important and that it provides satisfaction to him.

The hope of providing more self-actualization to the employee of the future will come about by the creative redesign of jobs that will build into jobs the opportunity to partake of the decision-making process and the opportunity to use imagination, creativity, and ingenuity, which are widely and not narrowly distributed in our population.

Two theories hold hope for the future: Chris Argyris' job enlargement, or horizontal job-loading theory, in which we string together a number of tasks of similar complexity with the hope of increasing employee motivation by reducing boredom; and Frederick Herzberg's job enrichment, or vertical job-loading theory, in which we design jobs of increasing complexity. To date, these theories have not been translated to any great degree into practical and widespread use in industry, primarily because they don't guarantee that the job will be done better with the same or less cost. These obstacles will have to be overcome if we are to provide challenges and not under-employment to our misfits.

In the Motivator Hygiene theory, Frederick Herzberg makes the point that, although the hygienic factors of wages, fringes, working conditions, etc., are important, since their absence produces dissatisfaction, the way to motivate employees is to concentrate on the nature of the job itself, which can provide the employee with self-actualization, recognition, growth, achievement, and potential. Too much of industries' resources have been spent on the hygienic factor and too little on the motivators or satisfiers. That is Herzberg's way of laying down the gauntlet to industry for the future.

As a final statement, let me make the point that misfits are unhappy people; good fits are happy people. If you were to look up the definition of happiness in a philosophic dictionary, you would learn that happiness is the exercising of your spiritual energies to the maximum, and that doesn't necessarily mean getting on your knees and praying, but rather it suggests that happiness is a result of being able to utilize our God-given and acquired talents to the fullest. A system that provides for less cheats us all. It remains a challenge of the future for all of us collectively, education, government and industry, to provide the means for each one of us to reach for happiness.

DISCUSSION

Chaired by speaker Daniel Knowles, the management panel included:

Thomas Conley, Personnel Representative, Grumman Aerospace Corporation
Nan Dietrich, Jesuit Program for Living and Learning
Carroll G. Kitts, Manager, Employee Benefits, AIL, A Division of Cutler-Hammer
Philippe Scholten, Director of Placement/Employee Relations, European American Bank

Audience:

I am a guidance counselor and I think your remarks about guidance counselors were not constructive.

Mr. Knowles:

I thought I was being constructive by saying that guidance counselors, in order to be certified, ought to serve an apprenticeship so they know what they are talking about. I have gone out of my way in terms of setting up summer programs for guidance counselors so they can get a better appreciation of industry's needs. In some instances, a guidance counselor really grasped something that he could bring back to the school system. But, frankly, most of the guidance counselors who worked in industry during the summer complained about how tedious the work was, how hard it was to stand on their feet, how hot it was working in a factory, and so on. So my personal experience with guidance counselors who have come into industry hasn't been all that good.

I have had too many cases of guidance counselors, for instance, telling young women not to go into engineering because it's man's work; too many instances of guidance counselors urging young women to become beauticians when there are not enough such jobs open; and, too many instances where a counselor doesn't even know what kind of remuneration can be gotten in different types of jobs. I don't think, in general, that guidance counselors pay much attention to the work-bound. I don't think they really do their homework in the world of work, the real world of work.

Audience:

I am interested in knowing what industry is doing in terms of handling affirmative action programs.

Mr. Scholten:

Generally speaking, the banking industry has provided stereotyped positions to certain segments of the work force. For instance, if you look at the general distribution of employees in a bank, you might see maybe about 40 percent male and 60 percent female. However, if you look at the distribution of the work, then indeed you will notice that a larger amount of females are in the lower levels of work, you don't see many male tellers or male secretaries. If you go upwards, then you indeed notice in the management levels a much greater number of males, white males. We are very aware of this and we are trying to combat this stereotypic work force distribution.

A number of years ago it was accepted that a male accountant must start at nine thousand dollars while a female accountant, no matter how bright she was, would start at six thousand dollars. That type of inequity in our bank has been rectified.

Now, in addition to this equal pay concept, we also look at the numbers of the affected class—to use a typical government term—those people who because of history, culture, or tradition may not have had the same opportunities as typical middle-class white males. We look at our training groups and we make an effort to see that a considerable number of all management trainees are members of minorities, including females. But, on the other hand, we have severe problems in finding numbers of professional minorities. In addition to our ongoing management training programs, we also do sensitivity training. If a department head asks for a receptionist and says she should be good-looking, we say, why "she" and why "good-looking?" We are not only training people for better positions, we are also making our middle management more aware.

Audience:

I would like to know if your company has a program for the troubled employee, specifically for the employee who has an alcoholic problem.

Mr. Conley:

Yes, we do have a program. Depending on whose statistics you are looking at, the rate of alcoholism in industry today runs somewhere between 5 percent and 10 percent. With approximately 22,000 employees, we feel that our investment in this type of a program will be returned to us. Our approach to this problem is to look at alcoholism as it relates directly to work performance. Our 2500 supervisors have just finished an orientation program on the disease aspect of alcoholism. The supervisor, in dealing with the troubled employee, does not mention the word alcoholism; performance is the criteria. We have set up a system of referral where an employee requesting help, or needing help, does have that help available within the company or outside the company.

Mr. Kitts:

I am pleased that this question was raised because it gives me an opportunity to explain how our company's program evolved.

About six years ago, we started an alcoholism rehabilitation program; we brought speakers into our company and impressed on all of our supervisors the need for bringing alcoholism problems to our attention in the Personnel Department. (In Personnel we rarely see symptoms of alcoholism. The supervisor, however, is in a position to spot symptoms when they exist.) We established a relationship with South Oaks' alcoholism treatment program to which we referred those employees brought to our attention.

About three years ago, we decided to broaden and improve our program; we asked supervisors to bring, not only the alcoholic to our attention, but also to report any evidence of what he would characterize as abnormal behavior. We had found that when we asked the supervisor to bring alcoholism to our attention, many times what he referred to us as an alcoholism problem was, in fact, not associated with alcoholism at all. By referring all such cases to South Oaks for diagnosis, we find that our program is much improved. For example, we have had cases referred to us where alcoholism was merely one of several contributing factors to a person's abnormal behavior and, as a matter of fact, was the least of several symptoms of abnormal behavior.

When the supervisor makes on-the-job observations that seem to him to indicate a problem of any kind, he refers the employee to Personnel, problems such as failure to produce, failure to follow instructions, inability to get along with other people, and absenteeism (particularly when it follows a pay-day or a weekend). We now refer the individual as quickly as possible to qualified professionals.

Audience:

In view of the increase in young peoples' drinking, would you comment on what your group does in this area?

Ms. Dietrich:

Many of the young people who come into our program have a problem with alcohol. We find that with our home environment, with a psychologist and a Jesuit in residence, we are able to learn about underlying problems. With such a close relationship with the Jesuits and a family-living situation, our residents are able to get to the heart of their problems, including alcoholism.

Audience:

As a black man expecting to move upward in management, I consider myself a misfit because there are social and cultural aspects of the job that I am not familiar with and that management is not prepared to deal with.

Audience:

I know from my experience in the military that we did not send certain people to certain areas. And I know in business that people who miss vital parts of the whole management process do not progress as they should.

Mr. Scholten:

I have not seen any difficulties in placing minority members. I think there is too much emphasis being placed on color. I am convinced that if individuals are motivated and they want to get ahead, they will make it. Look at what has been happening to our society here in the United States. We see a great number of blacks in high governmental positions and in industry positions.

Mr. Knowles:

I think a couple of other words might be said about affirmative action. It is true that back in the 60's the conception of affirmative action started with the minorities, blacks, Spanish-Americans, orientals, and American Indians. Then, women became an affirmative action consideration. In addition, we also now file affirmative action plans for the handicapped. We are now required to have an affirmative plan for veterans of Vietnam. It is very likely that in the near future we will have to file plans to protect individuals between the ages of 40 and 65 against age discrimination. In the late 60's legislation was passed protecting people who were Catholics, Jews, Southern Europeans, and Middle Europeans.

To put this into perspective, guess which is the biggest group, the middle-aged worker and the older worker. They represent 45 percent of the work force in the country, followed by women, at about 40 percent, followed by blacks, at about 11 percent. I don't know of any statistics that have been validated as to how many handicapped there are or, for that matter, who would fall under the Vietnamese Veterans Act. Now what's it all about? I think it has one simple common denominator. Everybody wants the same thing, a fair shake; and that is why we continue to have special-interest groups. I think special things have to be done for people, but not as groups, rather, as individuals. There is a spectrum of thought, personality, temperment, and views on life within any group of people. Whatever is done should be done on an individual basis to meet the needs of the individual.

Industry looks for people who have the backgrounds to do the job. If you are looking for an engineer, you look for someone who has an engineering degree. If you are looking for an accountant you prefer to have someone who is an accountant. Now when it comes to affirmative action, we start to think in terms, not necessarily of people who are fully qualified, but of people who are qualifiable. That is really what affirmative action is all about. You have to make an investment. Affirmative action costs money for companies. It doesn't come free. It is an investment.

Audience:

There is a great deal of discussion in the country today as to whose province it is to help prevent problems such as alcoholism and drug addiction that people bring to the job. Do you feel that industry today has a responsibility in the area of prevention as well as the home, the school, and the church?

Mr. Conley:

Yes, but prevention is difficult. For instance, so far we find we are not getting the early-stage alcoholic. We are getting the so-called middle-stage and late-stage alcoholics. With the late-stage alcoholic, we have to assume that here is an individual who has been covered up for a long time. In many cases, these people really are not in a position to be rehabilitated. In terms of prevention, we believe that ongoing education is the key; we have educational programs for supervisors and also for non-supervisory personnel. The deeper we get into this subject, the more we realize that there is a tremendous amount of ignorance about alcoholism.

Mr. Kitts:

The company certainly has a responsibility to assist in staving off alcoholism or any other form of emotional trauma, but it must beware of invading an individual's privacy. A problem is none of the company's business until it surfaces in the work place. If you try to counsel an employee before the problem begins to affect his job, then you are invading his privacy.

Audience:

The American Medical Association defines alcoholism as a terminal disease that is totally treatable. Does management believe that or do they believe, once a drunk, always a drunk? Can a man advance within his company if he shows complete promise of recovery?

Mr. Kitts:

There is almost reverse discrimination in favor of the alcoholic who proves that he can get his problem under control. Once a man comes back and makes it, he is going to advance probably much faster than anyone else because everyone is so pleased for him.

Mr. Knowles:

That kind of an alcoholic has such missionary zeal, it takes five people just to keep up with him.

Audience:

I would say that most of us here have been misfits in industry at one point or another if we have been dissatisfied with the job we were doing.

Mr. Knowles:

We are in a transitional period, as I see it in industry today, in which companies are aware of social responsibility not only for affirmative action purposes, but in general to improve the quality of their workers' lives. Any time you go through any kind of a transition, something is going to happen. It will probably take to the end of the century before we see that greater change.

Audience:

Some of the greatest people in the world have been the worst misfits. Benjamin Franklin was one. Thomas Edison was another.

Mr. Scholten:

Industry today does have a large social responsibility, but we must remember that profits have to be made. If there are no profits, if the company goes out of business, then we will have even more misfits.

We have concentrated on the problem of the over-qualified person. But we must remember that we also hire people in our society who simply do not want to have more, who want to work only from nine to five, and who don't want to carry their work home. We have to accept that, it is part of the makeup of certain people. It is indeed our responsibility to enrich the lives of our employees, but again, many people are not interested in going upwards.

People who want to go on to other jobs should take some responsibility for their lives. They can go to night school. They can go to the supervisor and say, "Hey, I don't like this job, it's not providing me with a growth opportunity." It is up to the particular person to take initiative and not just feel sorry because he feels he is a misfit.

Audience:

What about the so-called "hidden" job market? Many jobs do not open up through the traditional means of agencies and ads; people have techniques of career opportunity research. What is the personnel department's role in hiring?

Mr. Knowles:

The internal employment process comes first if a company really has the interest of its employees at heart. If a job cannot be filled from within, then the personnel department looks outside the company.

I think that basically there are four ways in which people find jobs. First, if possible, they use personal contacts. Second, they comb the help-wanted ads. Third, are the employment agencies and consulting firms. Finally, they can solicit jobs at companies after doing some research, say through the Thomas Register or some other means of locating companies that do the kind of work they are interested in.

As for the "hidden" job, often the personnel department will circulate a resume within a company, when there is no job opening, because a supervisor or department head may see in that resume something special that does not exist in the company, and it gives him a creative urge to add a new dimension to his department.

Audience:

As a vocational rehabilitation counselor, I keep bumping into a "Catch-22" situation. Our job is to take emotionally, mentally, or physically restored people and help them get back to work. After training these people we find that, even in the fat years, employers are looking only for people with a minimum of five years experience. A young person who has just been trained is not employable. How should we go about getting jobs for these people who have been trained but who have little or no experience?

Mr. Knowles:
   To a large degree it depends on what is going on in the economy at any given time. If a company has few jobs open in the system, then it can afford to be highly selective. Then you can select that person with the one brown eye and one blue eye who speaks Portuguese and has a background in marketing. On the other hand, strictly from a pragmatic standpoint, as the supply dwindles and the demand is greater than the supply, you do the next obvious thing, you hire "greenies" and train them. Now, it is true that the first job in most professions is very difficult to get because everybody looks for somebody who is 28 years of age with 15 years experience. And that, by the way, is the biggest problem for both the middle-aged and the older worker.

Audience:
   The handicapped have these problems to a much greater degree.

Mr. Knowles:
   Right. That is why the Rehabilitation Act of 1973 was passed.

Audience:
   What are the guidelines we can get from industry, if they were to cooperate with us, as to what people should be trained for, what particular jobs might be coming up in the future?

Mr. Knowles:
   That really hits the nail on the head because that is the biggest single area where there is a need for communication between industry and the educational system, what people should be trained for. One of the problems is that manpower planning is a rather imprecise science. So much depends on the economy and the fluctuating supply and demand of the marketplace. For instance, the aircraft industry might ask you to train hundreds of people to be aircraft mechanics and then, much later, after you have them trained, tell you there are no jobs. A company that has the ability to forecast its business, accurately, in terms of manpower, has got to give the educational system some lead time. You can't train people overnight.

Audience:
   People at the top know ahead of time that there is a contract from the Federal government in the offing.

Mr. Knowles:

It works to a limited degree when you are going up. The problem is when you are coming down.

Mr. Kitts:

You have both a short-range and a long-range problem; how can you get people jobs, and what areas should they be trained in? I would strongly recommend that, to solve them both, you call any large company switchboard and ask for the EEO Compliance Officer. He should be able to answer both of your questions. He is also especially motivated to hire the handicapped because that is one of his principal functions.

Audience:

We have been told that there is a high unemployment rate for youths between the ages of 16 and 19. When I was growing up I stayed in school until I was 18. What is wrong with our educational system today? Why are kids out looking for jobs? When we talk about misfits and look for the area of responsibility, isn't it in our educational system?

Mr. Knowles:

In preparing people for work, teachers should not only teach kids to operate machines, they should be talking about the real nature of work, what it is like to stand on your feet for eight hours a day in a plant where the temperature can get up to 90 degrees.

It amazes me to see kids looking for jobs who come in wearing undershirts, not T-shirts, undershirts. Of course, we can blame the family too, but we can also blame an educational system that during the whole 12 years, didn't even care how students went to look for a job. You dress up in a suit, maybe you even get a haircut, or at least wash your hair, and come in and look presentable for a job. After all, we have to respond to each other's needs. The person who is doing the hiring, whether it is right or wrong, is in the catbird seat. If a kid wants a job, he is going to have to respond to the needs of the guy who has the opening, because that is where the power is. It is just common sense.

As a matter of fact, my own behavioral theory suggests that we in industry don't have the resources to be able to change the way people feel; we can't change their personalities and their temperments, and all the training in the world within reason, isn't going to do that. We know that a person with emotional or mental problems often goes to a psychiatrist for years, at 50 bucks per 50-minute session, in order to learn to cope with life. Well, if it takes that kind of effort between the psychiatrist and the individual, then industry, in no manner, shape, or form, is ever going to reconstitute people. It is like shoveling sand against the tide. You can present new ideas that are compatible with their views and temperment and personality, but for anybody in industry to try and present a concept or an idea that is not compatible with the person's own views or temperment, forget it, you are really spinning your wheels.

So where is the answer? Since you can't really change the way people feel, it is important to change their overt behavior by modifying your overt behavior to meet their needs. Managers must understand the importance of establishing a good rapport with their employees, that this rapport makes good business sense on an intellectual level. The manager has got to be able to modify his overt behavior to meet the needs of that employee. What does that suggest? It means that you are going to use velvet gloves when you deal with that shy, reticent, introverted employee. If you don't, not only are you not going to establish good rapport, you are going to have a problem employee. The converse of that is also true. An easy-going boss who has a hard-nosed aggressive employee working for him will have a hard time establishing a relationship until he realizes that the only thing that the employee is going to recognize is strength. Unfortunately, there are people you have to hit on the head with a two-by-four to get their attention and that means taking the velvet gloves off. I like to think of it as being sensitized in terms of meeting the needs of others.

CHAPTER 4
The Primary Physician and the Problems Seen with the Mis-Employed

MAURICE GOLDENHAR, M.D.*

I am slightly perturbed by the term "misfits." It may well define the question at hand, but it has a pejorative connotation; one visualizes individuals who are devoid of certain qualities or abilities or who have physical or emotional handicaps. It may well be true that as a result of misemployment, some individuals' masked problems will erupt and many will seek medical help. The vast majority of these will turn to family physicians.

What is a family physician? How does he differ from the general practitioner? What is his role to be in the sphere of medical health? For those who have not followed the evolution of family medicine, permit me to recount what has occurred since 1969. Prior to that date, a number of far-sighted individuals, observing the steady attrition in the ranks of the generalist, made

---

*Maurice Goldenhar earned his M.D. degree at the University of Geneva, Switzerland. From 1954 to 1976, Dr. Goldenhar was in private family practice in Nassau County, New York. Since 1974, he has been associated with the Department of Family Medicine at the School of Medicine of the State University of New York at Stony Brook; at present he is a full-time Assistant Professor. Dr. Goldenhar is also the Director of the Department of Family Practice and the Family Practice Residency at South Nassau Communities Hospital, Oceanside, New York. He is a Consultant in Family Medicine at the Nassau County Medical Center, East Meadow, New York, and the Franklin General Hospital, Valley Stream, New York.

some wise decisions and created a new specialty, family medicine. As such, it had to fulfill the requirements set down for specialty training and obtain the proper credentials from the AMA accrediting bodies. This was accomplished in 1969 with the creation of the American Board of Family Practice and today over 10,000 physicians are diplomates of that board.

A core curriculum was devised at the undergraduate level and for residency training and, as of February 1977, there were 310 such residency programs in the United States. I am certain that the full impact of this revolution in medical education for primary care will not be felt for a number of years to come.

Though considered a specialty, family medicine is different in that it aims to deal with the physical, emotional, and social problems of entire family groups, from the cradle to the grave, and to strive to improve the quality of life between these two milestones. As physicians of first contact, the family physician is the conduit into the vast conglomerate called "medical care." It goes without saying that the preparation for this role, a 3-year training period, will provide the future physician with the ability to handle most problems that he will be asked to treat. It will also make him keenly aware of other more crucial situations which will require specialty opinion and therapy. But it will be the patient who will reap the benefits of this continuous and comprehensive attention to his needs. It is a recognized fact that a majority of complaints for which patients seek advice are problems in which the psyche plays a major role. Therefore, training in the behavioral sciences is fostered and, with the assistance of concerned psychiatrists, greatly encouraged.

In the past, the generalist, or general practitioner, usually launched his medical career after one year of internship, with little preparation in medical school for a vast group of psychological problems and, somehow, with a lack of confidence in psychiatry and at times, even distrust. But he did and still does possess a well-developed sense of caring and dedication. It is the fervent hope that the latter two qualities will be inherited by the new family physician.

To quote Stewart Wolf: "It is helpful to consider the individual as a living system entirely dependent upon maintaining a satisfactory relationship with his total environment. It is equally essential for him to maintain a satisfactory relationship with other human beings, and especially with those who, by kinship or long association, have acquired a special meaning to him (1)."

He further states that man needs to derive spiritual nourishment from his activities and the things that happen to him; and he needs to satisfy in some way his various emotional yearnings, including his unquenchable thirst for power and prestige; and to realize his potential for love and for creativity. Threats to his ability to perform in all of these spheres constitute the important everyday stresses that are apparently behind so many states of disability and disease. He concludes that preventive emphasis in medicine demands that we take into consideration all of these factors, and that we attempt to develop satisfactory ways of dealing with them individually and collectively.

Work is an integral part of most adults' lives. It affects attitudes on the job and at home, and it is often a determining factor in defining the general level of satisfaction, or dissatisfaction, with life. It contributes to self-esteem in two basic ways: People feel competent when they master the challenge of work; and they feel competent when they think others consider that they are doing something of value. So it is not the specific job, but the dynamics of working that is important for most people.

Ideally, having a good job means doing interesting work, using acquired skills or developing new ones, supervising others, or being permissively supervised. These factors tell the person who is working that he or she is important, useful, and appreciated. They also help develop a sense of autonomy. Other determinants of work satisfaction include good pay, promotions and job security, the development of good personal relationships, and the successful completion of a job well done. A key to good mental health is adapting to work in an organization without losing a sense of humanity. More and more men and women are insisting that work involvement, management styles, and employment opportunities be improved to enhance their sense of identity and feelings of individuality and competence (2).

Bertil Gerdell (3) maintains that severe restrictions of worker freedom and control, and in qualifications required, are found to be related to increased work alienation and lowered level of mental health. Walter Reuther, the late president of the UAW, maintained that lack of involvement at work is a major contributing factor to absenteeism and poor work performance.

Medicine has a social duty which it cannot escape. The actual functions of medicine in society extend beyond its avowed functions. In industrial societies this avowed function is at the organic level, to cure and prevent disease. But it is quite evident that medicine has an additional function at the personal level. This is to reassure and to allay anxiety in individuals, whether healthy or diseased, who in their distress turn to the doctor.

In industrial societies, the sick are dealt with by a vast and growing system of medical care. This modern burgeoning of medicine has gained its strength from an armament of technical facilities and treatments, and these are controlled by ever-narrowing specialisms based on discrete organ systems or on particular technical expertise. Yet, at the same time, the bounds of medical competence have been extended, and medicine deals increasingly with personal and social problems. Its implicit terms are to adjust the capacities of individuals to the complicated behavior demanded of them by society (4).

Not infrequently, however, doctors succeed in communicating instructions to their patients but often fail in communicating reassurance of information about disease. This is one of the lacunae that we are striving to overcome.

In some industries exposure to chemicals and other hazards will take a toll of a small number of the work force, but a larger number of workers will suffer very deeply from chronic dissatisfaction with their work, whether it is caused by lack of reward, monotony and boredom, unsuitability of the work itself, or failure to achieve satisfying status. Some studies have shown that prolonged monotonous work impairs a worker's ability to think and makes him likely to show childish emotional responses. His visual perceptions become disturbed. In some, hallucinations may appear and, in others, EEG patterns have been shown to change.

Boredom may set in very insidiously and it may be very difficult to recognize its onset. People suffering from boredom will often drive aimlessly; many over-indulge in alcohol and other drugs; others may sit listlessly watching TV and overeating.

Alcoholism has permeated all stratas of society. Stressful events for some individuals find their solution in a round of drinks. Soon this becomes a habit and many find themselves at a hopeless impasse. They alienate their friends, estrange their wives, and come into conflict with the law for a variety of reasons. At times, there may be a renewal of enthusiasm for one's work, and some achievements, but when faced with dissappointments there is a renewal of alcoholic drinking.

The ultimate mis-employment is unemployment. Its affect on physical health and mental health and a corresponding increase in criminal aggression, was shown in a recent Congressional study. In the five years between 1970 and 1975, there were 1500 suicides and 1700 homicides, all related to unemployment. All ages, both sexes, and whites as well as non-whites, were represented.

A recently published book entitled "The Angry Middle-Aged Man—The Crisis of America's Last Minority," (5) is an interesting study of men who have become unemployed at a time of life when they really should be the beneficiaries of the promises of the American Dream.

Certain periods of life have a very crucial effect. Each one of us has a personality structure stamped with neurotic attitudes and patterns from childhood and other stages of life. When new situations arise, causing repetitive frustrations and stresses, the resulting problems will depend on the severity of the core neurosis and the effectiveness of defensive and compensatory patterns in keeping the basic neurosis under control. But in middle age, some of these defense mechanisms somehow are overtaxed. The most critical psychosocial stimuli result from changes in the family structure and relationships, and from changes in vocational status. Thus, in the real world, losses and gains may become sources of stress to most people but, to certain types of neurotic personalities, the problems may have a more profound impact with the development of a whole array of physical symptoms.

The middle-aged compulsive worker, promoted to a supervisory or managerial position, may have trouble delegating work or may impose compulsive work patterns which cause unhappiness in his subordinates. He may drive himself so hard to do the work that he creates for himself a variety of problems of both an emotional and possible physical nature.

In the treatment of these individuals who do seek help, it is important to uncover for them the interaction between realities and neurotic tendencies and to help them cope more satisfactorily with the basic needs and the new problems prescribed by the events of middle age.

In the middle years there is a great demand for adequate emotional adaptation during a rapidly changing period of life (6). The problems include psychosocial, sexual, and psychological conflicts. Awareness of the physical aspects of aging becomes a reality. There is a gradual decrease in gonadal sufficiency associated with neuroendocrine imbalance, and varying emotional reactions are underlying factors of the psychosomatic problems (peptic ulcer), sexual difficulties (secondary impotence, frigidity, extramarital affairs), and psychological problems (hypochondrias, depressions, breakdown of marital relationships). Treatment of the patient in this involutional period requires that the individual be allowed to develop a controlled dependence upon the physician. In turn, the physician must remain sensitive to the problems of involution and encourage the patient to talk about his feelings.

Some hidden changes in levels of catecholamines, uric acid, and cholesterol occur months before signs of peptic ulcer, hypertension, or heart disease begin to appear. In dealing with such symptoms and in searching out their causes, physicians should consider how, and if, the patient is coping with the stress of work. Some occupations, by the very nature of their demands, lead to greater incidents of illness; air traffic controllers, when contrasted with people in less stressful jobs, are shown to have higher rates of hypertension, peptic ulcer, and diabetes. It is important to be aware of the over-dramatization of illness; some people do not tolerate half-measures, they must be either all well or totally sick; others, eager to maintain self-esteem, will demonstrate inability to work because of illness.

It has been widely claimed that the majority of patients seen by primary physicians, especially generalists and family physicians, are seeking help for significant emotional problems. Different individuals will perceive reactions to events with a gamut of different reactions. Many with similar problems will not seek professional help for they will have been able to call upon reserves and to restructure priorities and thus eliminate stumbling blocks.

It is prevention that we must seek, prevention of the development of full-blown threats to one's mental health. This prevention is bolstered by the physician who encourages individual coping competencies, by devising alternative courses of action, and by exploring more positive ways of using abilities. There is no definite therapeutic pattern that will fit everyone. The physician should be able to employ a variety of therapeutic regimens which will prove most effective in each instance.

The emotional problems that patients bring to their primary physicians are often masked by such symptoms as headache, backache, numbness, abdominal pains, etc. Encouragement on the part of the physician to discuss these emotional problems is most salutary as it permits the patient to open a Pandora's Box of repressed experiences. Proper interviewing techniques are thus very important. It is also important to bring out positive personality resources to enhance the problem-solving behavior of distressed patients. Family physicians are in an advantageous position as they already have the condifence of the patient through past and sometimes very lengthy relationships, and an intimate knowledge of the family's strengths and weaknesses. Involving the family in the problems of its members may be most productive and may even shorten the course of therapy, which at first looked quite protracted.

Depending on the specific situations, people who have experienced similar stresses may be asked to give a helping hand. Mutual self-help groups (AA, Al-Anon, etc)are often very helpful in working out emotional problems for identically afflicted individuals. Thus, the primary physician is able to place at the patient's disposal a number of problem solving schemes which may bring some solution to a variety of problems.

The telephone is important to the physician, though at times he wishes Alexander Graham Bell had never lived. Depressed patients don't take much time on the phone, usually two to three minutes, just to report in. I think they feel secure knowing that at the end of the wire there is someone who shows interest.

Some physicians, generalists and specialists alike, have not yet accepted the fact that physical complaints are sometimes the harbinger of deeper emotional strife and thus, they miss depressive states, especially if these depressive states are "masked." (We know that a significant percentage of suicide victims have sought medical attention within the immediate few weeks preceding the act.)

At the same time, I do not wish to leave the impression that all complaints voiced by patients are solely psychogenic. The physician must investigate fully. First, the investigation will show the patient that his problem is being treated with interest. If the diagnosis uncovers physical findings that are ominous, further support will have to be provided. If, however, the investigation shows that a psychological problem is the main cause, then appropriate therapy and direction may be given.

When mental disorder is analyzed, it reveals that psychoneurosis, as well as psychoses, is more prevalent among people in the lower economic scale. Schizophrenia rises sharply in this group, expecially in large cities. Multiple causes have been suggested for schizophrenia; these include not only psychological, biochemical and genetic factors, but social factors as well.

Schizophrenia is especially common in unskilled and unmarried young men. Two main hypotheses have been advanced to account for this social class distribution of schizophrenia. The first, the "breeder" hypothesis, is that the disease arises in special social circumstances and is particularly associated with social isolation of the individual. The second, the "drift" hypothesis, is that schizophrenic patients drift down to the unskilled occupations as they find themselves increasingly unable to hold down steady jobs and, as a consequence, live in neighborhoods with low social prestige. Schizophrenic patients had occupations of low prestige that frustrated any aspirations they might have shared with the dominant culture to upward social mobility. Schizophrenics in such areas live separated from the domestic support and personal relations that families could afford them. Employees in the lower levels may feel more frustrations from limitations inherent in their work.

Brenner, in "Mental Illness and the Economy" (7) states that economic instability is found to be one of the most pervasive and continuous sources of stress in industrialized society. Economic decisions or factors which increase instability and unemployment sharply increase the level and rate of mental hospitalization. He further states that the young and elderly are the most expendable members of the society at a time when emotional and financial resources are in critically short supply. He notes that there are two stages in a working man's life, the passage from "apprentice" to "qualified worker" and then the passage from "qualified worker" to "senior worker" or "official." For males, the sharpest impact in an economic downturn results in the privation of the opportunity to progress beyond the relatively junior stages of a career and also the opportunity, later in life, to progress to the top. His final conclusions are that economic downturns bring about increases in psychiatric symptoms as well as an intolerance to mental illness.

A number of authors, among them R.R. Fieve (8) and D.F. Klein, (9) have made the observation that depression is a common mental ailment. One in 20 Americans will be medically diagnosed as experiencing depression at some time during his or her life. They most often will approach their family physician rather than a psychiatrist. Many patients will go to their doctor with somatic complaints, obscuring or coexisting with an underlying depression. Thus, it becomes the family physician's responsibility to diagnose depression and, in all but the most severe cases, to treat the patient. It is important to give adequate time (several 20-minute-sessions), for interviews to allow the patient to open up and begin discussing his or her feelings. In some instances, with the patient's permission, consultation with relatives may have to be resorted to. The physician should be attuned to the possibility of suicide in depressed patients. It is mandatory that the physician ask questions about thoughts of suicide or previous aborted attempts. It is important to remember that the risk of suicide in these patients may increase during the early phases of treatment, when there has been a partial response that involves an increase of energy and motivation, but not an associated improved mood.

Some pitfalls to avoid in diagnosis include: not obtaining an in-depth medical and emotional history, not consulting with the family, missing an organic basis for depression, and mistaking anxiety for depression in the agitated patient.

As to therapy, the physician must be aware of adequate dosages for maximal effect. The adverse effects of drugs must be known fully for they may affect the cardiovascular system, producing conduction problems and drops in blood pressure to undesirable levels, with accompanying fatigue. The patient should be warned of anticholinergic side effects such as dry mouth, constipation, difficulty in urinating, etc. The practitioner should be aware that about 30 percent of patients with depression may not respond to tricyclics. When chemotherapy is withdrawn, it should be done gradually, with reinstatement if symptoms reappear.

As far as psychotherapy is concerned, the physician must be optimistic about the treatment, and give guidance and support. It may be wise not to refer to a psychiatrist for long-term therapy until the acute episode is under pharmacological control. During this phase, the initiation of intensive, long-term psychotherapy may further demoralize the patient by accentuating his or her feelings of inadequacy.

However, referral must be made for patients with suicidal tendencies, (especially if they live alone); for patients who react adversely to drugs; for patients in whom certain drugs are contraindicated, those with severe and recurrent depressions; those in the manic phase of a bipolar disorder; those who become manic in response to antidepressant therapy; and those who have complicated psychological factors associated with their depression. In "Fear of Success," (10) a psychiatrist, Dr. Leon Tec, makes some important observations. Fear of success can be caused by the unconscious thought that success will lead to failure in another area. A person may unconsciously fear that the "success" is not justified and that he is a fraud. That person might refuse a promotion outright, or accept the promotion but become so emotionally paralyzed that he cannot function in the new job. Success means change and change is always unsettling. Sometimes a person's self-image does not catch up with his professional competence. In these cases, it is important to place the self-image into line with reality. Dr. Tec also observes that as women are able to succeed more readily in the business world, more of them exhibit fear of it. For women the problem is even more complicated by the factor of competition with men. At the same time, men are rather intolerant of a successful woman. He concludes that if success really will mean more hardship than a person is prepared to put up with, the game may not be worth the candle after all.

As to the question of over-training and mis-training, I do not believe that easy solutions are at hand. A recent series of articles (11) investigating the job market for recent graduates, revealed that only one out of eight geography majors worked in his or her chosen field; and only eight out of 31 majors in sociology, 16 out of 49 English teachers, and 62 out of 160 elementary teachers, worked in their chosen fields. Thus a large number of people were either unemployed or employed in positions for which their college studies did not train them. Most likely they were over-trained. It goes without saying that frustrations, anxiety, and even depression may develop in some of these people.

Despite reports of widespread layoffs among teachers, policemen, and social workers, thousands of students continue to work towards those careers. This situation has caused concern among occupational counselors.

In partnership with psychiatrists, psychologists, sociologists, and social workers, as well as leaders of industry and the labor movement, we must help launch a campaign to minimize the effects of boredom and overwork, as well as all negative aspects of modern technology.

REFERENCES

1. Wolf, S. (1971). Patterns of social adjustment and disease, in "Society, Stress and Disease" (L. Levi, ed.), Vol. I. Oxford University Press, London.
2. "The Question of Coping" (No. 9). Hoffman-LaRoche, Inc., 1975.
3. Gerdell, B. (1971). Alienation and mental health in the modern industrial environment, in "Society, Stress and Disease" (L. Levi, ed.), Vol. I, Oxford University Press, London.
4. Susser, M.W., and Watson, W. (1971). "Sociology in Medicine" Oxford University Press, London.
5. Watters, P. (1976). "The Angry Middle-Aged Man—The Crisis of America's Last Minority" Grossman-Viking Press, N.Y.
6. Steiner, B.W. (1973). "The Crisis of Middle Age" Vol. 109, pp. 1017-1020. Canada.
7. Brenner, M.H. (1973). "Mental Illness and the Economy" Harvard University Press, Cambridge, Massachusetts.

8. Fieve, R.R. (1975). "Physicians Guide to Depression" P.W. Communications, Inc., New York.
9. Klein, D.F. (1977). "The Physician's Handbook on Depression" A Guide to Office Diagnosis and Management, Pfizer Laboratories.
10. Tec, L. (1976). "The Fear of Success" Readers Digest Press, Thomas Y. Crowell Company, New York.
11. (1976). College and Careers, *Newsday,* July 17.

DISCUSSION

Chaired by speaker Maurice Goldenhar, M.D., the panel of physicians included:

Penny Budoff, M.D., Assistant Professor, Department of Family Medicine, School of Medicine, Health Sciences Center, State University of New York at Stony Brook
Luther Cloud, M.D., Assistant Vice President and Associate Medical Director, Equitable Life Assurance Society of the United States
Daniel Friedman, M.D., Associate Professor, Department of Family Medicine, School of Medicine, Health Sciences Center, State University of New York at Stony Brook
Gottfried Lehmann, M.D., Medical Director, The Long Island Rail Road

Audience:
I have an employee who has a drinking problem, and my problem is that this particular employee refuses to seek help.

Dr. Cloud:
Does this employee's drinking problem affect his job performance? Your organization is not paying him to be absent, to be late, or to be uncooperative. There is an assumed contract between this man and your organization. You pay him a wage and he, in turn, performs his job satisfactorily. If he is not, you have a right to say to him, "I cannot tolerate your absenteeism; therefore I am suggesting to you, either you get help yourself or let me get you help, or in three months you will have a second review and, if at that point nothing has been done, I think we can dispense with your services." If that does not work, you have to be willing and ready to put into practice what you said.

If the man says, "Well, I don't really think I have a drinking problem but if you are so set on it, if you want me to get some help, what kind of help do I get?," you can't come up with egg on your face and say, "Well, I don't know." You must know what is available in the community, counseling, hospitals, clinics, AA. Your job is to motivate him to get help. If this man had a cardiac condition and you encouraged him, motivated him, to go to a cardiologist, you would not prescribe the digitalis and you would not look at his electrocardiogram. What you do is motivate him.

Dr. Lehmann:

We have indirect means of finding out that an employee may have a drinking problem. His performance record shows that his work is not as good as it should be; he is coming in late and has frequent absences for unrelated illnesses such as gastritis and colds. If the supervisor has been trained to recognize a pattern, then we will be able to help the employee. We also get referrals from co-workers and through the unions. Should the employee have an alcohol problem, we give him a complete physical examination after which he is referred to our alcoholism counseling program with appropriate recommendations and instructions for follow-up visits to the medical department.

Dr. Goldenhar:

Do any of you have any experience with the use of, or abuse of, certain drugs and substances such as marijuana and what effect they may have on jobs?

Dr. Cloud:

Whether it be marijuana or mainlining heroin or sniffing glue, or whatever, if it interferes with the job function of an individual, this is reason for intervention. If it does not, this is not a reason. We are today, very rightfully, extremely conscious of civil rights, individual rights. In the privacy of my own home, if I drink too much, this is not the business of my employer. But if I come to work and I am unable to function, or if I jeopardize the reputation of my company, then this my employer's business. If our people are in line with the national average, then probably 30 percent to 40 percent have smoked marijuana at some time or another. As long as this does not interfere with their job function, it is none of our business. However, if the use of a drug does interfere with the job, then this is reason for both management intervention and medical intervention.

Audience:

Diabetics and former cardiac patients, after their seizures, often need counseling to help them handle their new limitations.

Dr. Goldenhar:

Cardiac patients certainly can receive a lot of support from their own physician, if the physician will take the time. In many communities there exist "heart clubs" formed by people with heart diseases. They get together to discuss their problems brought on by their condition and how to overcome them. Diabetics have an organization which can provide them with information which will help them cope with their jobs. In certain hospitals, nutritionists, dietitians, and nurse specialists in diabetes help them with certain of their problems.

Dr. Lehmann:

I want to comment on the patient recovering from a cardiac episode. His body image has been destroyed and he has to rebuild it and maybe even modify it. The more mature the person, the easier this can be achieved. During this process, the physician provides medical supervision, assurance, and guidance. But a physician just does not have the time to spend hours and hours counseling the man as to what kind of activities he can do and how to reshape his life. This is the function of a social worker or of some kind of social agency. By the same token, there are a multitude of medical and social services available in the communities of which the physicians are unaware because there is no structured network of communication.

Dr. Friedman:

In my experience with the two diseases, heart disease and diabetes, industry by far has been more tolerant than governmental agencies. Perhaps the biggest blow to their ego that these patients encounter is when they have to reapply for a driver's license. They have to prove to governmental agencies beyond a shadow of a doubt that they are qualified. The necessary proof sometimes is unreasonable.

Audience:

Individuals that I have come into contact with, and their families, are often very depressed. They must be reassured because they seem at a loss and wonder if they can ever perform again in their jobs.

Dr. Goldenhar:

My experience over the years has been that the problem becomes less and less as time goes on. In fact, after the first birthday of a heart attack, you see a rejuvenation. They need a tremendous amount of support during this period of time.

Dr. Budoff:

I think that the doctor has a tremendous responsibility with this type of patient. For the coronary patient, rehabilitation begins right in the coronary care unit. Patients who have survived that first 24 hours, that first milestone, need reassurance. I think it is important that the doctor be optimistic. My patients get prepared to get back to work, period. They know they are going to be home in two to three weeks and that you expect them to climb stairs and you expect them to return to a normal sex life and you just expect this of them and you tell them this. Patients often don't ask you things that they might like to ask you and I think the physician has a real responsibility to tell patients what they ought to know.

I don't think there are many jobs that a patient could not continue after heart surgery unless he does heavy labor or is a pilot, for instance. The pilot who has a coronary, that's it, he must look for other employment, perhaps within the aviation field, but he is not going to be flying 747's again. But, lawyers, doctors, blue-collar workers, white-collar workers, all go back to work after a coronary, and right from the beginning they should know that you expect them to function.

Audience:

They have to be reassured that after they get over the recuperation period they will be able to get right back to work. Not just their doctor, others must tell them too.

Dr. Cloud:

Every one of our physicians has in his office a form which is called a short-hour form. It has been printed to help people coming back to work after illness or injury. For instance, a person isn't required to come in at nine and meet the midtown traffic; he or she comes in at ten and leaves at four. Hours can be changed to a certain extent. We are very conscious of the needs of the patient. We are continually in touch with the private physician who must tell us what the patient can do. We also recognize emotional stresses. It is my job to know what an employee is returning to when he returns to work. For example, we sell insurance and every once in a while we have a drive. Now, I don't want a myocardia employee coming back in the middle of that pressure. I know his family physician doesn't. By talking it over we can say, let's keep him out another three or four weeks until the pressure is over. Or, let's bring him back and tell him, you're not part of the drive this year, we don't want you working late every night. The fact that we have forms printed up means it is not the exception, it is the rule.

Dr. Friedman:

The type of patient who is a big problem to his wife and his friends is the one who tries to do everything immediately.

Dr. Goldenhar:

Dr. Budoff mentioned sexual aspects. Men usually will question the doctor prior to leaving the hospital about sexual relations. Women usually don't, except one, many years ago who the day before she left said, "How about sexual relations?" She took me aback and before I had time to answer she said, "Yes, I know what you are going to tell me. Only with my husband, so I don't get excited."

Audience:

I am a social worker and I work in the field of mental health. I have had patients who have had to be hospitalized for, say a couple of months and many of them, when they leave the hospital, have to try to look for different jobs, and they are asked if they ever have had a mental illness. I question the morality of this question.

Dr. Lehmann:

Let me answer this question indirectly. We do not feel that sending an employee to a psychiatrist is admission of mental illness of any kind. We send him to a psychiatrist because we feel that the psychiatrist is the most apt person to provide proper counsel and evaluation. Unfortunately, our intentions and objectivity are often misunderstood and misquoted because of the label attached to psychiatric care. A psychiatric evaluation is not synonymous with mental illness; on the other hand mental treatment should be considered in the same manner as an organic illness.

Audience:

I think that companies feel safer in dealing with employees who have had physical ailments than they do with employees who have had emotional problems.

Dr. Lehmann:

This depends on the type of industry and job responsiblities and the kind of illness. If an employee's job, prior to his mental illness, was to drive a train which carries passengers, we will not return that employee to a position where he is responsible for those passengers, unless we are absolutely certain that he will be able to discharge his responsibilities by meeting all criteria and standards of care and efficiency. An epileptic with breakthrough seizures, on the other hand, would not be able to drive this train any longer. An employee never loses the right to own his job as long as he is physically and mentally capable of performing the duties pertaining to his job.

Dr. Cloud:

A new law on nondiscrimination in hiring is giving those of us in occupational medicine a very hard time because it is saying you cannot categorically deny employment to anyone provided he or she can function. If an individual, diagnosed as having a manic-depressive psychosis, who has spent weeks, months, or years in a hospital, is functioning at this particular moment, we do not have the right to deny him employment. By Federal mandate, we do not have a right to deny employment, despite the fact that this might entail a tremendous risk.

Now, if we do not have the right to deny them employment, we do have the right to try to fit them for employment. I saw the movie, "Taxi Driver;" I don't want to ride in the back of a taxi with some schizophrenic like that. On the other hand, manic-depressive personalities, and obsessive-compulsive personalities make the best secretaries in the world. So we do make adjustments. I don't want the epileptic we were talking about driving a company car or flying an airplane. But an epileptic young lady, who occasionally had mild seizures, was able to work in our library without any problems.

One of our jobs, and I think this may be the clue to this entire conference in a sense, is to place people in what we consider to be the very best circumstances for them and for society at large. We have got to consider risk factors for the community as well as the rights of the individual. But the rights of the individual, as far as I am concerned, must always be considered first.

Dr. Lehmann:

We examine a person to find out if this person is medically qualified to hold the position applied for. Management makes the decision as to whether this person has the necessary skills, experience, aptitude, and potential, and selects from a pool of similarly qualified applicants. Nowadays, no one is refused employment for medical reasons, be he an amputee, be he blind or be he a cardiac cripple. The point is, he must be able to perform the job at the moment and not endanger the safety of others.

Dr. Cloud:

In other words, you should put down the truth because the truth will be found out anyway.

Dr. Lehmann:

If you omit a vital fact requested on an application and you acknowledge that you have provided all the information which was requested by signing your name, then this omission can become an issue and result in your dismissal for falsification of records.

Dr. Cloud:

With the truth we can do far better in assessing what round hole to put a round person in than if we are working with a mixture of information, supposition, and rumors. If a prospective employee has spent three years in a state hospital, those three years have to be accounted for. So he was three years in a state hospital, the idea is he got better. This is much better than disappearing off the face of the earth. It is important to have facts.

I think we have to admit that what we are trying to do is find a place for an individual because I don't think any of us is stupid enough to think that when we don't hire someone that we do anybody any good. Because if you don't hire him you pay taxes for unemployment, or if you keep him in a hospital, you pay for that too. So what we all want to do is to have people employed to the best of their functions, and that is the catch, to the best of their functions.

Dr. Budoff:

In my practice I get into the problems of working women. I hear about emotional problems that are caused because the women work at night and their husbands work during the day. It is very time consuming to deal with those problems, and I am not a psychiatrist, but I do it because I think it is important. It is important to listen and to ask questions. "How crucial is this job to you if it is giving you ulcers?" "What is this job really worth to you?" "What would be the risk to you of changing jobs or just quitting this job?"

People get themselves into binds and sometimes need someone to help them sort out their problems.

Audience:

What kind of advice do you give your patients who, because of disability, must change their jobs?

Dr. Friedman:

We'd have to know what is the age of the individual, what is the training of the individual, what is the attitude of the individual, what is the experience of the individual? We all talk about how difficult it is for heart patients to return to an occupation; in my experience it is much more of a tragedy for an individual who has had a stroke and is paralyzed on one side.

Dr. Budoff:

Changing jobs may not always be bad and I think this is one point that we missed. You can look at the horse from either end and maybe it is time to take a look at yourself and what you have been doing for the past 20 years. Maybe because of your illness, you will find something more exciting. Maybe you won't have the same boredoms, you'll have new boredoms.

Dr. Cloud:

People will hang on for dear life to a bad job. But you have to set priorities. There are people who, after recovery from a stroke, will drag themselves through the wind and the rain and the cold to get to a job when they could probably be rehabilitated to be something at home that they could do very well.

Audience:

How about nurse practitioners? Are they being hired by management so they can identify troubled areas before they erupt?

Dr. Goldenhar:

Some of the insurance companies are using nurse practitioners in this sense.

Audience:

I handle compensation cases for an insurance company. I coordinabe home care and make sure there is proper medical management. One of our greatest problems is very poor doctor-patient communication. I constantly get calls for explanations of treatment plans. I feel this is the physician's job.

Dr. Goldenhar:

We are trying to educate our residents and give them evidence of these deficiencies so they are aware of the importance of spending time with their patients, explaining the reasons for medication, and explaining the causes of disease.

Dr. Cloud:

On the confidentiality issue, it is all right for a private practitioner to send a claim on his patient to the medical director of the company. It is not all right to send it to a third party. It is not all right to send it to the personnel director for it to become part of a personnel record. Patients have a complete right to confidentiality whether they are treated by a nurse practitioner, a social worker, or a physician. If a claim comes to me as a medical director, I am also bound by my own confidentiality and I am not going to send it to the personnel department. I will adjudicate what I think best on the particular case. But all too often the patient is caught in a bind. He won't get paid, so says the company, unless his doctor sends in a form. The patient then asks the doctor to send it to his boss, or the director of personnel. This means it now becomes part of a verticle file that spills all over the place.

Dr. Friedman:

We now have the question of what medical information is available to computers. This is certainly a great threat today. The biggest problem is with Medicare and Social Security and how capable they are of keeping information confidential. A recent survey indicated they cannot control the roots of their information.

Audience:

As a physician I am concerned about confidentiality in terms of how it relates to what we put down on an insurance form, especially in cases of mental illness. Are we doing our patient a disservice if we specifically detail the information that an insurance company requires, and which will probably keep him from getting his policy?

Dr. Cloud:

I do not think it will necessarily mean that the employee or the patient will not get his insurance policy. For example, an alcoholic, contrary to what most people believe, can get insurance. Of course, an active alcoholic, a drinking alcoholic, can no more get insurance than somebody who has just had a prostatectomy. Nor should they, because the risk factors are tremendous. But after a year a recovered alcoholic begins to be rated as a premium, and there comes a time where a policy is sold to a recovered alcoholic at standard insurance rates.

An individual who has a psychiatric history, who has been hospitalized and treated and who can give you a period of time, which is adjudicated by clinical experts, in which he is doing well, is exactly the same as an epileptic who indicates that for two years he hasn't had a convulsive attack and is taking medication under the direction of a doctor. Facts are not nearly as harmful as secrets. If a person falsifies his medical history, and then is hospitalized or dies, the entire policy can be declared null and void, as though it never existed.

Audience:

May I extend the question further? I have had patients in the hospital for psychiatric disorders whose bills are being paid by the insurance company. Often a request will come in requiring rather specific, detailed information which goes beyond the chief complaint and into some of the collateral history, which makes it very difficult for us to answer. Very often the insurer will not honor a claim simply because this information is not supplied; and we feel very strongly that the confidentiality of a specific issue about this patient should be kept within the framwork of the hospital. Somehow I feel the company and everybody and his brother gets his hands on it.

Dr. Cloud:

That information, if it is directed to me or the medical department, is as confidential as it is in your hospital because we are bound by the same confidentiality as you are.

Audience:

A physician should release information only to another physician.

Dr. Friedman:

There have been cases where the employer has sued the doctor and won the right to get information from him. The doctor is obliged to the employer, not to the patient. That physician has no right to withhold information from the people who pay him.

Dr. Goldenhar:

If he did withhold it, he wouldn't have the job for very long.

Audience:

The company physician has a primary obligation to protect the company's liability. As such, the man making management decisions has a right to information he needs to make employment decisions. Confidentiality does come up, but that is secondary to protecting the company from liability.

Dr. Cloud:

We are talking to two different things. I agree with you a thousand percent. Many times I help management make decisions, but that is different from turning over my medical records, or that they can be by law taken away from me.

Audience:

I see many so-called misfits in industry who are certainly not over-educated or over-employed.

Dr. Cloud:

Many of the minorities in our industries are misfits, but not because of over-education, or because of mental illness, or because of broken bones. I sometimes deal with the minorities that come from black communities and Hispanic communities in Manhattan and Harlem, two groups who have been among the most disadvantaged of any group. I see 17-year-old, 18-year-old, 19-year-old young men who have finally gotten a job, usually because of affirmative action. Up until this time in his life no one has ever expected that young man to be on time for anything. His mother and father didn't care if he got up on time to go to school. Maybe his father was drunk, maybe his mother wasn't there. The teacher certainly didn't care if he came to school; if you've got 116 people in a class and 16 don't show up, that's 16 you don't have to worry about, so you are not going to go out and look for them. All of a sudden this young man gets a job and his boss says, "I want you here at five minutes to nine tomorrow to deliver the mail." What does he care about five minutes to nine? Nobody ever expected him to be on time for anything. He's been conditioned by society to be a misfit long before he starts the job.

Audience:

I am an industrial nurse and my firm employs many young people. We see a great deal of teenage drinking. How should we cope with it?

Dr. Cloud:

If you see an increase in your company of people with suspicious chest X-rays, what are you going to to do about it?

Audience:

Refer them to a physician.

Dr. Cloud:

Well, I think you have your answer to what to do about teenage drinking.

Audience:

I don't actually see them drinking. It's word of mouth. But I do know they call in sick on Mondays.

Dr. Cloud:

You treat them the same way you treat a 55-year-old alcoholic. You are not doing your job, you are absent, you're late, it still comes down to exactly the same thing. The teenager happens to be someone under 18 but you don't treat the problem any differently.

Audience:

Will they eventually become misfits in industry?

Dr Cloud:

Also misfits in life. An alcoholic, and I am not talking about a heavy drinker, I am talking about a person who is diagnosed as being addicted to alcohol, will remain addicted to alcohol as long as life is made easy for him, as long as everybody lets him, as long as everybody gives him the money, as long as he is forgiven, as long as the wife cleans up after him, as long as his boss pats him on the back and promotes him. But as soon as somebody begins to say, you have responsibilities, then we begin to make inroads.

CHAPTER 5

Problems of Education
and Employment

WALTER S. NEFF, Ph.D.*

The issue posed by this conference concerns the mental health problems of the individual who is over-educated but under-trained for the kind of employment that is available. Included here is an implication that there is a serious lack of congruence between the education process and the requirements of gainful employment in contemporary society. More exactly, there is an inference to be drawn that there may be a significant number of people in our society who spend more time in school than the work they may ultimately perform actually requires of them, and who may, in the course of their schooling, acquire aspirations, hopes, and lifestyles which they will not be able to satisfy on the basis of the work ultimately available to them. Assuming this sort of gap or discontinuity between education and employ-

---

*Walter S. Neff earned his M.A. in philosophy at the University of Pensylvania and his Ph.D. in psychology at Cornell University. Initially trained as an experimental psychologist, he became interested in the social psychology of mental disorder when he served as a psychologist in the armed forces during World War II. His major research field has been the social psychology and psychopathology of human work. Dr. Neff has taught at a number of universities, including the University of Chicago and New York University. During the 1960's, he developed (at NYU) one of the first doctoral training programs in community psychology and community mental health. Currently, he is Professor Emeritus at New York University and Professor of Psychiatry (Psychology) at the School of Medicine of the State University of New York at Stony Brook.

ment, can we expect some sort of exacerbation of mental health problems? Can we go further and make any recommendations for educational policy or, indeed, any recommendations concerning social policy generally?

This is a very large and serious question, and we have very meager data with which to attempt some kind of answer. The first aspect of the question that we must face up to is the question of fact. Is there, in fact, a developing problem of this kind? Is there an increasing number of people in our society whose education and potential unemployment are out of sinc and who are therefore doomed, permanently or temporarily, to frustration and dissatisfaction with their work? It is certainly possible to come across individual cases which fit this pattern. All of us who are engaged in the practice of psychiatry and psychology have patients whom we can think of in these terms. All of us have read or heard horror stories of skilled engineers working as bartenders. We know that colleges of education are curtailing their activities because of an alleged over-production of teachers. We are told that we are turning out too many lawyers or too many computer technicians. Are these disasters the consequence of temporary dislocations, like the collapse of the aerospace industry after the withdrawal of government funding? Or are these long-term secular trends, which tell us that something is seriously out of kilter in social planning?

In order to get some sort of fix on this problem, we need to step back and take an overall look at the educational enterprise itself. The United States is the classic country of mass public education. We started it earlier than other countries. We made it compulsory and universal before anyone else. It is probably no exaggeration to say that millions of immigrants came to our shores with the aim of securing an education for themselves and, especially, for their children. We have always regarded it as the indispensible requirement for the good life. We spend enormous sums for it and commit to its operations the lives and resources of millions of people. Are we now saying that it is possible to get too much of a good thing? Are the aims of the school and the aims of society generally moving in somewhat different directions?

What is schooling for? This question has been asked by every generation and has received a bewildering variety of answers. Every society we know of has evolved some sort of procedure for educating its young, but none as complex and intricate as our own society. Are the schools designed to produce competent workers? Good citizens? Cultured people? Adjusted personalities? Skilled technicians and professionals? Literate individuals? What? The school has evolved in our country to the status of a major social institution and, like other major social institutions, is called upon to meet the needs of all our people, although in fact it may be maximally useful only to some. There are important educational authorities today who believe that the educational establishment is being asked to do too much and is consequently blamed when it does not achieve all that it is asked to do. It is instructive to read one of the more current lists of the aims of education. As stated in 1966 by the American Association of School Administrators, the basic imperatives of our educational system are as follows:

1. To make urban life rewarding and satisfying
2. To prepare people for the world of work
3. To discover and nurture creative talent
4. To strengthen the moral fabric of society
5. To deal constructively with psychological tensions
6. To keep democracy working
7. To make intelligent use of natural resources
8. To make the best use of leisure time
9. To work with other people of the world for human betterment

In passing, I shall make only three observations on this official listing of educational objectives. First, we are obviously a long way from the "Three R's." Second, the obligation to prepare children for adult work is only one of many obligations, although we note that such an obligation ranks pretty high. Third, we might well ask if we have not assigned to the schools a set of tasks which makes their basic mission (assuming there is one) virtually unachievable. It would appear that we have abdicated to the educational system a set of responsibilities that were once thought to be the prerogative of more primary social agencies: the home, the family, the church, and the like. By requiring the school to achieve too many goals, will we end by discovering that it can do none of them very well, and that its original objective (the transmission of knowledge and the inculcation of cognitive skills) has somehow been lost in the shuffle? If we now conceivably face the problem of the over-educated, can be blame the schools, since, like any other social institution, they are guided by the principle, the more, the better?

Who is to be found in the schools? Well, these days, practically everybody. Some comparisons are noteworthy. If we go back 200 years, only a tiny minority of the country's children received any kind of formal schooling; today, in the age group 6 to 13, the proportion of children in school reaches 99 percent. If we go back 100 years, only a small minority (approximately one in seven) of our young people entered high school; today, upwards of 70 percent actually graduate from secondary school. When it comes to higher education, all comparisons fail. The latest figures show that upwards of 50 percent of college-age youth enter some sort of post-secondary school education or training, of whom about half complete a baccalaureate program. Whereas the 4-year college was once the stamping ground of an educational and social elite, it is now itself virtually a mass-education enterprise.

What are the reasons for this enormous expansion of formal education, much of which has taken place during the past couple of generations? Obviously, one of the primary causes has been the enormous technological progress of the present century and the demands of an ever more complex and intricate society. But this is by no means the sole cause of educational expansion. A society that regards itself as democratic can hardly deny educational democracy to all of its citizens if it is available to some. Not the least significant aspect of current pressures for increased egalitarianism has been the entry into middle and higher education of increased proportions of such population sectors as women and ethnic minorities.

But in addition to these rather obvious and well-accepted causes of educational expansion, there is another powerful force which is less discussed. I am referring to what could be called the inner life of education as a major social institution. Once major social institutions come into existence, they have a way of perpetuating themselves and even growing without much regard for their original reasons for coming into being. People develop powerful personal and social investments in the institution with which they happen to have primary involvement and these investments are not easy to undermine. There also develops what could be called the tyranny of the expert. The insider claims expert knowledge and the non-specialist is increasingly being thrust into the position of being unable to decide upon policy. Like other major social institutions, the educational enterprise has increasingly developed a life of its own and has strong tendencies to operate according to its own requirements and needs.

So far, we have said a few things about education, but very little about the other term in our equation: the world of work. Human work is an extremely complex set of activities, with a very intricate history, but I shall here confine myself to one overriding issue: the problem of gainful employment. The question we are trying to grasp then becomes somewhat narrower. What are the relationships, then, between formal education and the actual labor market? Are these two systems generally congruent or are they, in certain respects, out of phase? Do our schools adequately prepare our children to carry on, as adults, in the ever varying types of paid employment that now exist in contemporary society? Is there, in fact, a segment of our population which can be said to be over-educated and under-employed?

From one point of view, to ask this question is to answer it. The preparation of young people for employment is, as we have seen, described as a major goal of education. However, whether this goal is to be seen as an aspiration or as a justification, it seems fair to say that it has never been a particularly realistic objective. In the early days of the republic, schooling was confined to the winter months, when the demand for agricultural labor was at a minimum, and the organization of our school year still reflects this rather distant past. Today the chief, if not sole, occupation of children 6 to 16 is schooling, which has become, to a very considerable extent, an end in itself. The primary grades prepare for high school. Secondary education prepares for college. College prepares for graduate education and for the profession. The system is largely self-contained.

This is not to say that I am arguing that there is no relation whatever between the world of education and the world of work. some very important things take place during the school years which serve somehow to transform the playing child into the working adult. But these have more to do with the quality of the entire school situation than they have to do with the acquisition of any particular set of educational skills. Many of the requirements of the work role are first encountered in the school environment.

We have contended elsewhere (*Work and Human Behavior;* Chicago, Aldine Pub. Co., 1968), that the basic distinctions between work and play, and between work and love, begin to take shape in the mind of the child during the periods when he is forced to leave his family and his playmates for hours at a time to attend school. The child gets his first really serious conditioning to the clock; he is required to be at school on time, to stay a fixed number of hours, to go to lunch and return from it, to divide the day into school time and play time. He is compelled to accommodate himself to all sorts of strangers (his teachers and school mates) with whom he cannot really behave as he may continue to do with his parents and relatives. The child's schooling begins the long process of erosion of the ties that bind him to his parents, a process that ends in the more or less independent existence of the working adult.

Above all, the atmosphere of the school demands work, not play. Certain basic components of the work personality appear to be formed during the school years: the ability to concentrate on a task for extended periods of time, the development of response patterns to supervisory authority, the limits of cooperation and competition with peers, and the meanings and values associated with work. School is thus a precursor of adult work and provides a set of models for it. It may be gratifying, even useful, if a child enjoys his homework, but enjoyment is not the purpose of the process. Basically, the schoolchild finds that he is required to be productive, to be serious, to meet standards, to turn out a required amount of work at a required level of quality, to meet certain responsibilities.

But, and this is a very big "but," these relationships of school to work are very general and quite indirect. Nothing is said about the content of what is being taught. If we look for more direct relationships between what is actually being taught and the kinds of work people will do, we begin to get into difficulties. What the schools do best is to provide for the acquisition of cognitive skills and of knowledge for that sector of our youth which expects to enter the more intellectual and professional occupations. And this is where the prestige is too. The rewards and sanctions within our educational system are focused on intellectual achievement. Educational success implies movement through higher and higher levels of an intellectual process.

But what of the large majority of our children who will spend the bulk of their working lives in occupations that require very minimal cognitive skills and very little of the information and knowledge which the school imparts? I think that we will have to concede that there is not much of a direct relationship between what is taught in our schools and the kinds of work that the bulk of our population is required to perform.

There are many intricate problems here and it is easy to be schematic. For example, vocational education does exist and it is a not inconsiderable part of the educational system. There are vocational high schools which feature training in the more skilled trades and occupations. There is an increasingly large network of community colleges, which tend to focus on technical, rather than merely academic training. There is even a current great debate among university faculties that is turning around charges that liberal education is being eroded and that the colleges are becoming increasingly vocational in nature. However, we should note that the term "vocational" has many meanings and not all of the various parties to the controversy are using them in the same way. Unfortunately, although recently there has been some increased support for vocational training, the vocational high school is still, by and large, a dumping ground for the academically inept. Again, while there have been interesting efforts to develop two-year technical training programs in our community colleges, one in four of the students who enter community colleges are intent on academic preparation for transfer to a four-year college. At the college level, the debate over the virtues and vices of the classical liberal arts program is largely instigated by the demands made by graduate and professional schools for more specialized education.

Although vocational education, by that title, is something of a second-class citizen in the world of education, it is worth our while to take a closer look at it. In doing so, we shall need to broaden our conception of it. Narrowly defined, as it is mostly today, vocational education comprises those institutions which are geared to the production of people who, it is assumed, will enter the skilled manual trades and certain of the lower-level technical occupations. It is this sort of education that is generally found in the vocational high schools and in many of the two-year community colleges that are springing up in many parts of the country. The curriculum in these institutions is generally concrete and there is a great deal of emphasis on practice. Among some educational authorities this sort of thing is not thought of as education at all, but rather as "training." The implication is that education somehow involves theory, while training involves practice. Thus, the laboratory technician who graduates from a community college program may know what to do if asked to analyze a urine or blood sample in a hospital laboratory, although his general knowledge of blood chemistry may be minimal. The emphasis, of course, is on doing!

Yet there is a certain sense in which the most prestigious kinds of higher education are quite vocational in nature, although they are rarely described by this label. An engineering school, a law school, or a medical school, has a great deal of highly specific information to impart and is intent on training its matriculants in some highly concrete skills. The curricula of these institutions also typically feature a great deal of practice under supervision. We are all aware that the medical school today cannot really function without a satellite hospital, in which learning by doing, under supervision of course, is an integral part of medical education.

The professional school assumes that its matriculants have already received whatever general education that the academic high school and the four-year college have been able to impart. Their concern is to turn out a qualified professional, an expert in a particular occupational field. There are, of course, intense controversies about how this should best be done. There is concern that the typical graduate may be too specialized, may for example, know too little about general medicine, or about the influence of social institutions on health practice. But these concerns have to do with how well trained the graduate will be to function in his particular occupation. They are not concerned with how much the graduate knows about English literature or Latin American history. Nor, actually, should they be. Taking into consideration the enormous division of labor within the educational industry, this is really someone else's job.

Thus, understanding vocational education in its wider sense, graduate schools, colleges of education, and professional schools are as vocational in their nature and aims as is the vocational high school. The differences lie in the technical complexity of the occupations concerned, the value that society places upon them and, here we approach the crux of the question, the intellectual abilities required. But, like the vocational high school, their aims have nothing to do with the acquisition of culture or the production of good citizens. Their aims are to produce people who will carry out a highly specialized occupational role. Thus, their relationship to work is quite immediate and direct. Whereas the primary grades, at best, prepare pupils for the academic high school, and the academic high school, at best, prepares students for the academic college, the vocational high school and the medical school are alike in preparing people more directly for a working life.

Our brief tour through the jungles of American education has led us, I think, to a rather surprising conclusion. Despite the protestations of our educational policymakers, and despite the fact that we live in a highly work-oriented society, it does not appear to me that our schools really prepare our children for entry into the special world of paid employment. We exempt from this bald statement, of course, the rather derogated vocational high school, at one extreme, and the graduate and professional schools, at the other. The bulk of our education prepares children for more education! Whether the majority of our children are able and willing to continue with more and more education is another issue, and here a raft of social and economic factors play a major role.

I should hasten to add that I do not myself believe that this is a bad thing, nor do I see how we could arrange things very differently. With all its frictions and difficulties, with all of its apparent waste and inefficiency, to whatever degree, there are not too many Johnnies who can't read. I believe that the achievement of mass public education is one of the great glories of American democracy, and should be extended rather than contracted. I think that it is a scandal that in other great democratic nations, England and France, for example, higher education is still largely confined to a social and economic elite. It is no small tribute to the pervasiveness of our own democratic structure that mass education, even at higher levels, has taken on the character of a natural right.

There are disjunctions, of course, and the disjunction we are now considering is that between the world of education and the world of work. But perhaps "disjunction" is the wrong word. It is rather that in highly complex societies, different sub-regions of the society begin to lead lives of their own, begin to develop their own unique requirements, their own bureaucracies, their own standards. It is historically true that, at one time at least, business, industry, and agriculture had a much closer concern with what went on in the schools than they now appear to have. Industry needed a literate labor force; business needed vast numbers of clerks and bookkeepers; agriculture needed huge quantities of technical know-how. As a result, trade schools, schools of commerce, and agricultural colleges came into existence and played a direct role in supplying the world of work with new recruits. Once in existence, these specialized institutions increasingly led lives of their own. However, these special schools never comprised more than a rather small sector of the general educational system. Education in the United States has undergone its enormous expansion largely in terms of its own dynamics and in relation to social needs that have been largely unrelated, except in the most general sense, to the specific requirements of the world of work. Instead of speaking of a disjunction between the world of education and the world of work, it would be more accurate to say that the relationships between these two social domains are rather indirect.

Can we, or should we, do whatever we can to make these relationships more direct than they appear to be? Should we educate people more directly for the actual jobs they will perform? Shall we go still further and educate only those numbers and kinds of people whom we know in advance will be employed in a given set of prescribed jobs? I am afraid that to ask this question is to answer it, or rather, to ask it leads to the uncomfortable discovery that there is no intelligible answer. Social and economic forecasting is still a quite primitive scientific tool. It is simply not yet possible to sit here and say that in the year 2000 we will need precisely x numbers of doctors, lawyers, social workers, engineers, skilled electricians, or production workers. Also, with an extremely rapidly changing technology, we have no real way of knowing exactly what it is that all these future workers should know. All this is quite apart from the catastrophic influence of wars, revolutions, and major social changes, which can make rational social forecasting something of a mug's game.

There are some long-term trends about which we can be fairly certain. We know that the birth rate has been declining and, in the industrialized countries at least, may be in process of bottoming out at a figure approaching zero population growth. This in turn suggests that we will have relatively fewer schoolchildren to teach and this in turn has led to worries about a current overproduction of teachers. Of course, even this kind of calculation is subject to such issues as class size, the extension of education to segments of the population now entering the education race, and the possibility that education will continue during the lifespan rather than being confined to the so called school-age years. We know that the death rate has been declining too; that we, as a population, I am speaking of the United States, are living a decade or two longer than we did a few generations back, that millions of us will survive for many years past the present time of formal retirement from the world of work. This is currently leading to much speculation about the uses of leisure, about the kinds of work (paid or unpaid), which should be made available to an aging population, and even plans for the alteration and extension of traditional educational sequences.

Within the world of work also there have been some very basic changes of a long-term nature. Farm workers comprised the largest sector of the labor force only a few generations back; now, agriculture is the smallest labor force sector and is decreasing proportionately every decade. Within industry itself, there has been a massive shift from primary production to service, communication, and sales. Within the sphere of industrial production, the onrush of technology has tended to eliminate, at one extreme, the unskilled manual laborer and, at the other, the highly skilled journeyman craftsman. Thus, the entire blue-collar labor force is increasingly taking on the character of semi-skilled assembly workers, who put together semi-finished parts. These developments have virtually abolished the apprenticeship system which for centuries was the traditional path of entry into the more skilled and independent forms of blue-collar work. They have also rendered redundant the masses of peasant labor who once were able to enter industry at its lowest point, unskilled heavy labor, and move up in it to the more skilled occupations. Incidentally, this change in labor force composition is also one of the reasons behind the increasing difficulties of the vocational trade school. It is no longer considered desirable or necessary to spend years learning how to be a generalized machinist or electrician. The basic demand is for people to service increasingly versatile and "clever" machines.

How does all this bear upon the problem of the "misfit" in industry? Can we expect large numbers of cases of lack of fit between the kind of education a person has undertaken and the kind of work he or she may find available? And, assuming a drastic lack of fit, should we expect to encounter numbers of persons for whom this discrepancy constitutes a serious psychological problem? Given the great complexity of the two systems, education on the one hand and work on the other, and given the fact that interface between them is far from direct, I think we will find increasing numbers of people whose education and work are out of fit. How serious is this problem? What are the remedies?

I think that the problem is more serious in the middle levels of education and work than at the extremes. At the upper extreme, the trained professional, if misemployed or unemployed, has many more alternatives open to him or her. An electronics engineer, extruded from the space industry, may try his hand at technical sales, may land a job in administration, or may take a stab at starting a small business. Moreover, since education, as we have seen, prepares one for more education, he may find it possible to go back to school and undergo retraining for a different specialty. At the other extreme, the assembly-line worker is widely admitted to be discontented with his work, but this has more to do with the present manner in which production work is arranged than it reflects a major discrepancy between education and achievement. But the middle level technician is often very narrowly trained and thus, given the vagaries of the labor market, can undergo rather serious misemployment.

In this total situation, remedies are not easy to come by, although some are being discussed. One of the most important remedies currently under discussion would involve massive changes in the current structure of the entire educational system. It is now widely taken for granted that education is pretty strictly for the young, coming to a formal end in late adolescence or early adulthood. Education is seen as a necessity for the young, but a luxury for the adult. Fortunately, however, there are now a few educational authorities who are entertaining second thoughts. There is some increasing recognition that the immense pace of technological and social change may force education to be a lifelong, rather than a youth-limited, enterprise. It should be possible for a person, who finds that he is miseducated for the work available, to return to education at any time that his life situation makes this desirable or necessary. The current educational budget crunch may make this sound like an idle dream, but I believe that there are currents at work which will eventually make this possibility more realistic than it now appears to be.

A second major remedy has to do with vocational education. It will not be easy to alter the current low prestige of the vocational school, or its status as a dumping ground for the academically inept. There are drastic needs for wide reforms here, and there is some indication that serious efforts to reform the system are under way. Here also, the system ought to be much more flexible than it is. It is especially desirable that vocational education ought to be readily available to people of all ages, whereas, it is now chiefly focused on the adolescent years. The Federal Office of Education is appropriating increasing sums for vocational education, as are some of the states. There is, however, plenty of room for improvement.

A third remedy needed bears upon vocational counseling. At present, vocational counseling has the status of an infant profession. It is precariously sited in the high schools and is often the first victim of educational retrenchment. However, as a profession, vocational counseling is expanding quite rapidly and there are signs that it is being taken more seriously.

A fourth possibility involves the development of training institutions by industry itself. At one time American industry pioneered in this sort of thing, but much of its efforts have been abandoned to the educational establishment. Although there are pros and cons here, there is plenty of room for creativity. American industry, which frequently seeks a social role, might well find it in contributing directly to the education and training of its required labor force.

Finally, we need wider recognition that there is, in fact, a problem here. It is a mental health problem, as well as an economic and social problem. The organization of such a conference as this one, around the theme of misemployment, is a sign of the times.

DISCUSSION

Chaired by speaker Walter S. Neff, Ph.D., the panel included:

Patrick Carone, M.D., Assistant Professor, Department of Psychiatry, School of Medicine, Yale University

Norman Goodman, Ph.D., Chairman, Department of Sociology, State University of New York at Stony Brook

Arthur Haggerty, Ph.D., Director, Graduate Program in Health Care Administration, C.W. Post Center of Long Island University

Dianne Knight, C.S.W., Director of Social Services, South Oaks Hospital

Dr. Goodman:

First of all, I think we must be reminded of the importance of work in most societies. When Sigmund Freud was asked what are the two most important things that a person needs in order to have a stable personality, he said, the ability to work and to love, *arbeit und lieben*. We spend more time at work than at any other single activity, with the possible exception of sleep; and obviously it is of central concern. Also, particularly in American society, education plays an essential role in our conception of a person. What education did she or he have? What are they doing with it?

The mismatch between our educational system and our occupational system is not new; it has existed for a long time. I would like to use an analogy to make this point clearer: Marijuana was used in this country for a considerable number of years, but it was not considered a serious social problem until increasing numbers of white, middle-class college students began to use it. The same thing, I think, is true of the central issue of this conference. There has been a lack of articulation for many, many years between the talents and training of people, on one hand, and their occupations, on the other. It is increasingly seen as an important social problem because it is now more relevant to that same generally favored segment of the population as in the marijuana example, white, middle-class males. When we talk about misfits in industry, we are placing the problem on the backs of individuals and diverting attention away from problems with the educational and occupational systems. What is it about our educational and occupational system that leads to so much frustration in the world of work? I think one of the major issues, as Dr. Neff has pointed out, is the contradictory nature of the goals in education. In elementary and secondary schools, and in most colleges, there is no clear and direct relationship between education and a job. It is relatively rare when such a relationship does occur.

Instead of talking about over-production of people, why don't we talk about under-utilization of people. Let's use teachers as an example. Instead of saying we're producing too many teachers, why don't we see that presently we have a remarkable opportunity to improve our children's education by reducing class size? What a wonderful opportunity to define productivity in terms of the quality instead of the quantity of the product, the level of education instead of the number of students "processed." And lastly, let's look at the source of the problem, not just the problem itself. When a child cuts himself, someone has to clean it and put the Band-Aid on; but someone also has to find out what caused the cut so that it doesn't happen again. Let's look at the educational and occupational systems, and not just the so-called "misfits."

Dr. Neff:

For a long time it was easy to say, if a person had deficiencies or was unhappy or miserable, that there was something wrong with him and to speak of his limitations. It was the old story of blaming the victim. Now we are beginning to look at incongruities and difficulties from an environmental viewpoint. Can we offer arrangements under which people can live so that their mode of life, whatever it is, might somehow be easier and less destructive? Obviously, tinkering with individuals is easier. We know how to do it, or at least we know what to do. We know what sequence to carry through. But the point that I have come around to in my professional life is that, in many respects, tinkering with people is similar to trying to empty the Pacific Ocean with a tablespoon. In addition to focusing on individuals, we must also focus on the larger forces (social, political, economic) that play such an important role in our lives.

Dr. Carone:

I agree with you. If somebody is continually being injured by an eggbeater because it is poorly designed, you change the design of the eggbeater. You don't put a special hand guard on the individual each time he uses the eggbeater.

Audience:

What about the problem of male menopause, when a man who is 40 to 45 suddenly realizes that if the world is going to be set on fire, it won't be by him. He has gone almost as far as he can reasonably expect to go, and it isn't what he thought it would be when he had all those bright expectations. This in itself creates quite a few problems.

Dr. Haggerty:

Today people are living longer and are retiring earlier and there is an opportunity for many people to have a second career. If a person, let's say, retires from the Police Department or the Fire Department at the age of 40 to 45, it is likely that he will have 30 more years of productive life, so it is not unreasonable to expect that he could prepare for a second career. Many military people when they retire after 20 to 30 years of service have formally prepared for a second career in another profession.

Dr. Goodman:

Once more we are blaming the victim. Once more we are asking the individual to adjust instead of examining the utility of the system. Let me suggest that the problem is no different than one of the points I made earlier and that is, what is it we expect from our school system? What is it we expect of a person in his or her lifetime? We now teach people to expect to strive to go onward and upward to bigger and better things.

By the way, in reference to the comment about the "male menopause," many men have never had the opportunity to "enjoy" the "male menopause" because they have not been going up, but going down or sideways. But for those who have been going up, there comes a point where they fear that they are about as high as they are going to go. They have done pretty much all that they are going to do that is new and different. And because we have taught them that that is not enough, that they must always do better, they may then have the "male menopause." How then to get back to braving the world?

At this point why do people believe that society expects them to go into bigger and better and newer things? There are limits to how many bigger, better and newer things are possible, particularly as the world changes and becomes more complex. What we should be concerned about is that people do what they can do in ways that make them, and the people around them, happier. The role of the "misfit" often depends on how we define what we expect of people.

Dr. Neff:

In my last eight years as a director of a doctoral program, I have been struck by the number of women who are coming back for Ph.D.'s. I also see all kinds of men turning up for doctoral degrees: ex-rabbis, ex-Army officers, a Jesuit priest. Now these are people who plainly had career ideas when they were younger and they have lived their lives a certain way for a number of years. Somewhere along the line something shifted. We are seeing increased flexibility in lifelong assignments, and we are seeing that it is possible to shift, and increasingly necessary to shift. Occupations become outmoded. Engineering specialties disappear. Specialties in medicine change. As jobs change and patterns of work change, there is an increasing demand for different kinds of capabilities and skills. We are seeing, and will continue to see, more and more people going back to school to become re-educated.

Ms. Knight:

If you go to college campuses in the evening you will see large numbers of adults who are already in the process of planning for new careers.

Audience:

High schools could provide opportunities for youngsters to do more in the world of work while they are in school: for example, a half day in school and the second half of the day in a field of interest as a volunteer. Credit could be given for the outside work. It would be a great opportunity to build toward a career rather than just the academic part of one's life.

Dr. Goodman:

On the one hand we want young people to be in school because we want to teach them the basic knowledge they'll need as responsible citizens, as adults. On the other hand, we see the need for a closer relationship between secondary school education and the world of work. We really must get our heads together and decide what it is we really want education to accomplish. What kind of programs, for what kinds of kids, with what kinds of effects? Should certain kinds of schools concentrate on certain goals and other kinds of schools concentrate on different goals? If so, we are asking for a different kind of educational system than presently exists.

Dr. Neff:

I think everybody here realizes there is a mass problem caused by the incongruity of education and work. We know there are a great many people who are either over-educated or miseducated for they work that they do.

Audience:

Schools must take more responsibility in giving students a more positive attitude toward work.

Dr. Goodman:

Why should the school be given the responsibility of developing positive attitudes toward work when, frankly, most of the attitudes toward work have already been developed in children before they get to school by seeing how their parents respond to their jobs?

Audience:

I think our kids look for a very positive life even though their parents may feel that work is basically pushing a button, something you tolerate.

Dr. Goodman:

Do you think that going to school can change that? Why do we try to make school all things to all people, teaching basic skills, imparting positive attitudes towards work, teaching the classics, providing information on alcoholism, and so on? Why do we load everything on the schools and then blame the schools for failing to do "their job?"

Audience:

The concept of upward mobility was a moral value as far as I was concerned when I was in industry. Now I see it as a myth and maybe it is a myth that a lot of persons cannot live up to. It is a myth that has affected some of my older children. They thought they were really guilty of not being able to make it like they were taught. They learned in their religious training that there was a work ethic; if you worked hard enough then you ought to have enough money to be comfortable. And if you did not have stature in the community, something was immoral about you.

Audience:

Onward and upward is an economic concept directed at us whether we like it or not. As for moral values, people who were perfectly satisfied to have reached their level of incompetency or competency have suddenly found that, immorally, there is an inflationary spiral. Our values are now being thrust upon us by global forces over which we have no control.

Dr. Neff:

I think that there have been important shifts, even in my own generation, in the emphasis we place upon work. Sure, we are all indoctrinated with competetiveness and all the rest. But one of the interesting aspects of the shortening of the working day and the shortening of the working week and the shortening of the working year is that, almost objectively, we don't have to be as completely immersed in work as we used to be. That doesn't say it is not the most important activity in our lives; but it is not like working from dawn to dusk on a farm and, if you didn't like being a farmer, too bad.

There are lots of people these days, writing books with big worrisome titles about the threat of too much leisure. They are telling us: Look, the working day's reduced; there will be six hours a day, not eight. Maybe there will be four days a week, not five. Look at all this time. We've got to make work for idle hands so we all won't go to pot because we haven't got this rewarding work to do. Well, there is something in it in the sense that nobody has ever explained to anybody or has educated anybody, that is consciously, about the talents of leisure. We have been educated how to work, but we have not been educated how to leisure.

I bet you that as the working day, the working week, the working year, decrease over time we will begin to want to educate ourselves for certain components of leisure and our values will shift. Work will not be an all-consuming thing in our lives. It is still terribly important, there is no doubt about that, because we no longer parade around talking about our lineage, or our national origins, or our religious beliefs as identifying characteristics. We are more easily identified by the kind of work we do or the kind of education we have than by anything else. Somebody asks me what I am. I am a college professor. How many times do we hear, what does he do? Work tends to identify us. But, sad to say, new problems are making their appearance and these problems have to do with values around non-working as well as values only in terms of work.

We are getting an increasing proportion of retired people in our population. By the year 2000 at least 30 million people will be over the age of 65. That's a lot of people. Do we have room in our ideology for unpaid work? Is it really work? Are hobbies work? Is volunteering work? Is it possible to work without being paid for it and still somehow recognize that a person can have an identity from it and everything else that work is supposed to bring with it?

Dr. Carone:

To my mind, it is a normal part of the human condition to be involved in striving and fighting and competing in various ways. I believe a certain amount of discomfort is part and parcel of being human. To my mind it becomes very important to make distinctions. What is normal striving? How much dissatisfaction is normal? What is it that drives a person to continue education, to continue seeking money? Beyond what point would the pushing become abnormal? At what point do you identify pathology? Why is the person so driven in seeking money; what is he compensating for that was missing in his childhood? What is missing in his life that he has to alienate everybody in order to amass money?

Where do you draw the line between the normal strivings and the normal unhappinesses, and the pathological ones? Somewhere the line has to be drawn. Where do you say that it is not the fault of the individual that he is unhappy, that the unhappiness he experiences is greater than that which is normal, and that society is responsible?

So to me there are three issues, three questions: How much discomfort and unhappiness is normal? How much does ambition and aggression play in this? Where does an individual become identified as suffering from some kind of psychological, emotional illness and where do you reach the point that there are so many individuals affected that it becomes a society-wide question?

The other issue which Dr. Neff was addressing, how to leisure, is very important. While visiting in Italy, I have been struck by the fact that, in that culture, leisure is a significant part of how time is spent. Unemployment and dissatisfaction with employment have been a part of Italian history for quite some time and a number of people have adjusted to this. Life on the piazza is a social institution. Several hours an evening are spent over a cup of coffee, meeting friends, talking, socializing. So there are cultures where people know how to enjoy leisure time.

But again, the most important point to me, is the distinction between normal striving, individual psychopathology, and societal psychopathology.

Dr. Goodman:

I want to forcefully, but respectfully, disagree with my colleague. I don't think that you can produce a shred of evidence to indicate that striving and achievement are a normal part of the human condition. There are many, many societies around the world where this is unknown. Variation is the natural order of things! On one hand you have the Ik, who will kill anybody in sight, their own children, their own relatives, their friends, who threaten their style and level of life. And those of you who have read Ruth Benedict's *Patterns of Culture* will remember the Dobuans, who are suspicious, aggressive, and never happy. Consider, on the other hand, the Zuni of New Mexico. They bar from further competition any man who wins more than once, because they simply will not tolerate individual striving or competition.

I think it is a mistake to build into the human condition what is a peculiar phenomenon of a particular society, or type of society, during a specific historical period.

Now that is not to argue whether striving is either good or bad. I think that it is perfectly appropriate to argue, as you did, that in our society there is a level of striving which is useful, but which, if exceeded, produces problems. But I think if we define this as part of the human condition, it leads us to avoid looking at the actual source of the problem: our society's expectations for achievement. It is very hard, I admit, to agree on what is an appropriate level of striving and achievement in American society. Given the structure of our society, the person who does not strive is generally seen as a misfit. What is "appropriate" striving is one of the issues we have to struggle with. I think, however, that the thrust of our society is to encourage most people to strive continuously, and this is not healthy. The "male menopause" is a nice example of the outcome of this kind of problem.

Dr. Neff:

There are basic changes going on. We are now beginning, during this last generation, this last quarter of the 20th century, to enter a period when conditions of work may be considerably different from what they were before, including early retirement to make holes in the labor force so that new ones can come in, including much shortened working days and shortened working weeks, and including, with the rapid development of technology, a major demand that we shift the kind of work we do. A good many things that we have talked about will look pale, because there will be revolutions in work lives. What do we do as health workers? Do you as health workers have any training to handle this situation?

Audience:

As a school nurse I work with youngsters. They are barometers of what is going on in the family. I can always tell when the father has lost his job or when there has been some dislocation, death, illness, or whatever. There has to be further use of medical people, other than physicians, who will go out in the field and identify these problems and help prevent ulcers and hypertension and nervous breakdowns.

Dr. Neff:

If there are these major secular changes, long-term changes, going on, isn't it highly likely that we are going to need more people who know how to deal with these issues? We are only beginning to take into account what so far seems to be almost an overlooked issue and that is that we spend two-thirds of our life and one-half of our waking day at work. And work involves so many contradictory issues. It seems remarkable that medical programs and social work programs and public health programs in our universities have almost ignored this entire vast area.

Audience:

I think we ought to consider a career monkey-bar situation in which a person may stay, descend, or travel laterally and still feel comfortable within the organization that he works for. If an executive finds that he is under too much stress, he should be able to move down into the company and still retain his salary and seek out a new career without penalty.

Audience:

I would like to go back to the point that Dr. Carone made about the piazza in Italy. I had a similar experience when I went back to Vienna. I was born there and I found that the coffeehouse was still intact where my father used to go to read his paper and talk. I made me realize that there is something we are missing and it isn't the piazza or the coffeehouse, it is the talking. We are so busy watching that we have forgotten how to talk.

Ms. Knight:

At work, we are often more concerned about our image than we are about really communicating with people. When we are able to interact with people in a warm, caring way, then we won't have to be concerned with images.

Dr. Neff:

We have ranged over a wide area, and that was perhaps inevitable, trying seriously to understand what human work is all about, trying to develop some psychological understanding of it. Of course our lives are not totally made up in terms of work. There are other aspects of life which have little to do with the kind of work we do and most of us take this for granted. Obviously our sex lives, our recreational lives, our cultural lives, our family lives, and so on, are not by any means identified with what goes on with work, though work may have an influence, one way or another. There are many aspects of us as human beings that are not to be exhausted by our summing up of human work.

However, I read a rather frightening Canadian sociological study the other day. It pointed out, with very good evidence, that the kind of work one does can also predict what kind of political activities, social activities, and personal activities one has off the job, and even to what degree one's recreational activities are a reflection of the work we do. Even in a single factory the blue-collar manual workers, the least skilled, the most uneducated, the most poorly paid, also have lousier marriages, lousier recreational lives, lousier everything. So there are many spheres of life that have to do with work. It is also true that the other spheres have some relationship to the kind of work that you do.

We hear very little about work in ordinary education. I think it is fair to say that nothing is told about work, it is taken for granted that you will work. One of the reasons for the so-called gap between school and work is that it is simply assumed that if you go to school and learn something you are also, somehow, mysteriously, going to become a satisfied and contented worker or a useful worker. This is not the case.

Until we all become more aware that working entails some rather complex social and psychological issues, we will continue to fumble in the dark.

CHAPTER 6

Labor Looks at
the Mis-Employed

SANFORD V. LENZ*

Allow me to start by quoting from the program for this conference on "Misfits in Industry": "For the first time in more than a generation people who work have had to cope with a situation where they were trained for a job and the job is not available. For the first time in the memory of most people we are confronted with a large under-employed population who have been over-trained or mistrained. This has brought on frustration, embitterment, discouragement and anxiety."

I say to you, not so, not at all "for the first time." In fact I say to you, we told you so, from the labor point of view. It may be a new experience for

---

*Sanford V. Lenz is a Labor Program Specialist on the faculty of the Extension Division of the New York State School of Industrial and Labor Relations of Cornell University.

He is an instructor in union administration, organizational behavior, labor history, and community services.

Mr. Lenz's labor background consists of 20 years as an elected officer of the International Union of Electrical Workers (AFL-CIO), including 10 years on the International Executive Board.

Mr. Lenz's extensive activities include membership on the Nassau County Youth Board, the Nassau Health and Welfare Council, the Nassau-Suffolk Comprehensive Health Planning Agency, the Board of Directors of the Long Island Labor Education and Community Services Agency, and the Federation of Labor Community Services Committee.

some professions—social workers, teachers, many public employees, and managers—but it is a very old story for workers. Don't tell us it's the first time. The 50 percent of the work force who are women have always had problems of working and being worked below their capability and below their training. Don't tell it to the minority workers—black, Hispanic, handicapped— who have, since we declared war on poverty, taken one training course after another only to find out that there were no jobs at the end of that line. Don't tell it to the employees of the Long Island defense industries for whom unemployment has been going since 1957 because of so-called "obsolescent skills." Don't tell it to the workers whose highly-skilled jobs in industry and in the construction trades have been destroyed by automation and by prefabrication.

In fact the American worker has always had the problem of frustration, embitterment, discouragement, and anxiety on the part of the unemployed and the misemployed. The labor movement has for some 25 years or more argued that unemployment and underemployment are two sides of the same coin. We have long argued and argue still that unemployment far exceeds published figures. When the figures say there are 9 percent unemployed, we say the number may very well be double that if you count those who have accepted part-time jobs or lesser-paying jobs or lesser-skilled jobs to keep some bread on the table, and if you count those who have been discouraged and have given up looking and who refuse to waste their talent and their training on "any old job."

Labor has consistently favored full employment as opposed to tax rebates, or expansion of unemployment benefits, or extension of welfare, or make-work jobs, for the simple reason that they know that when a skilled machinist takes a job in a luncheonette or a public service job cleaning parks and beaches, society might be terribly relieved; he is honoring the work ethic, their tax burden is eased, the unemployment figure went down, and he is not even eligible for food stamps anymore. But the impact on him as a human being is exactly the same as though he were still unemployed and on the dole. His self-esteem, his confidence in himself, is continually threatened. He might earn enough to pay the rent and to put food on the table but he must put aside what dreams he had, putting kids through college, or buying that little place in the mountains.

What does unemployment or underemployment do to a worker? The Brenner Report to Congress, the study by Dr. M. Harvey Brenner of John Hopkins which was made for the Joint Economic Committee, cited frightening statistice in terms of impact.

Every 1 percent rise in unemployment over a cumulative five years produces:

A 5.7 percent rise in homicides

A 4.1 percent rise in suicides

A 4.0 percent rise in mental hospital admissions

A 2.0 percent in rise in cirrhosis and cardiovascular mortalities.

Let me quote from the Brenner Report: "Unemployment," Dr. Brenner said, "has a self-evident meaning of loss of employment. Incorporated in the personal sense of loss, however, is the necessity of adapting to separation from fellow workers who probably constituted a major dimension of the person's closer relationships. The individual has an investment of training, seniority, and emotional ties to his work. These emotional ties are not only to persons but to the image of the job itself, since for a great many people the job defines the individual. Also lost is the opportunity for achievement that was potentially connected with the job. Hopes are destroyed and the individual is frustrated and anxious about the future."

What the labor movement has been saying is that everything in that paragraph is true even if the person finds some lesser employment. It has not changed one iota. He is separated from that job with which he was identified and with which he could identify himself. The fact that he found a job as a bartender or in a luncheonette or cleaning a park hasn't changed that a bit. Most interesting, though, is the summary statement that appeared in the report: "Unemployment plays a major statistical role in increasing social trauma," but it goes on, "we cannot assert a 'casual' relationship between unemployment and the various forms of social pathology." Let's stop a minute and see what that says. It says they can demonstrate that all these bad social things happen when employment goes up, but they can't prove that it happens to the people who are unemployed. While there are a lot more hospital admissions, it can't relate the physical condition of the people who are unemployed. This is exactly what labor has long argued. The disease called unemployment takes its toll among many others besides the person who is unemployed—his family, the worker who still has a job but whose security is threatened, and the person who is trained for, but unable to move into that job. It is reasonable to suspect that the social trauma works upon all those groups. The impact of teacher layoffs is felt not only by the laid-off teachers; it may have an even greater impact upon the students who have graduated from teachers college and found that society does not need 90 percent of them as teachers. What of the thousands of young people who are waiting anxiously for apprenticeship programs for building trades skills for which there are not, and in the near future will not be, any openings? The concept that being mis-employed has the same impact as being unemployed is not new to young people or indeed to academics. *The Journal of Occupa-*

tional Medicine in May 1967, that is 10 years back, reported a Cornell Conference devoted to "Mental Health in Industry" in a series of articles demonstrating the relationship between one's job and one's mental health or illness. A number of questions were raised then which deserve restatement.

Who is qualified to deal with the mental health problems of employees? What forces in the individual and in the organization are likely to precipitate latent behavior problems? What are the legal and private liabilities of management? What action can management and unions take to prevent and to treat mental illness related to the job? Many of the same questions and some possible answers were raised more recently in the publications of The Work in America Institute. The publications are called, "The World of Work Report," and I'll lean heavily on those documents from here on.

Let's first address ourselves to the question of which forces precipitate behavior problems. Dr. Alan McLean of N.Y.U. Hospital-Cornell Medical Center, said therein that what must happen is a coming together of three factors which must overlap to produce symptoms of mental illnesses in the occupational environment. The first is the environmental context of the job itself. Is it supportive or is it alienative? Is stress all around in the work place? Pressure always there, time always the enemy, clocks and calendars to be fought? If it is, that is strike one.

Second, how about the individual's vulnerability; his capability for coping; the general and developmental factors that measure how a person is going to react to stress? That is not really the question of just normal versus abnormal but instead is a whole span of vulnerability where some people are more or less ready to be easily affected by disturbances. If the person is in a state of readiness, that is strike two.

Third, are there risk factors around the job that act as immediate stressors or triggers? Crises, whether they occur at work or occur at home, can trigger emotional response. In case that happens in the presence of the other two, that is strike three and you are out!

Not everyone succumbs. Some people with low readiness can roll with the punches. Others have learned to shield themselves or to hide by changing the body chemistry to turn down the environment or tune up the body. I think it is safe to say that most of America does that. You might select alcohol, addictive drugs, caffein, or nicotine, but the odds are that you are into some combination of them. In any case, to reduce latent behavioral problems one or more of those factors must be reduced.

It should be obvious that we have very little control over the vulnerability of the individual. There is not much we can do about that from the outside. It should be evident that there is very little we can do to control or avoid the existence of the triggers, the crises that are going to arise. It appears to me, therefore, that the only thing on which we can have any impact is the environment, the work environment itself.

Let's look at a typical job representing one of the most difficult environments and, incidentally, involving primarily women—the airline flight attendant. The airline flight attendant has one of the most difficult and denigrating jobs one can have. She is trained, she is told, for safety, passenger comfort, customer relations, human relations, her ability to care for people; therefore, her job is important and requires competence and skill. It is the sort of thing people want to know about their jobs. But what are the facts about her job? Let me quote from a newspaper put out by a local union of flight attendants, currently in negotiations.

"What we are trying to negotiate is a change of attitude and opinion of our worth. Fifteen years ago this was a temporary job for many young attractive females searching for 'that man' on the white charger. Flight attendants, being predominantly female, have been regarded as subservient for eons, and we are still fighting the male dominance over our lifestyles. Times have changed and we have changed. We have a very real need to make it on our own and that must be recognized."

I'll leave out the name of the company but it goes on, "[the company has] let it be known that if we want a better way of life we shouldn't look to improvement in our jobs, we should find some man to support us. Failing that, to survive with three roommates."

Stewardesses are grounded immediately—and that means suspended without pay—if they get pregnant, if they gain weight, if they get sick more than three times a year, if they get stuck in a snow storm, or if they get a flat tire, also, if they wear the wrong shoes, if they get a complaint letter from a customer, or get written up by a ground supervisor, by a pilot, or by anybody else. "What other group puts up with that treatment?" the union paper asks. She must satisfy the demands of the Flight Services Department to sell more booze, she receives the brunt of pilot stress reactions, and she must smilingly accept the total boorishness of some passengers.

You know, traditionally it is railroaders who have gotten the reputation for alcoholism, usually attributed to the lonely layover in a remote small town. That small town consists of two rooming houses and a bar and you select from that your entertainment for the evening. Think of how the problem is compounded for an airline stewardess; not only is she subject to the same kind of layover but she is in charge of two suitcases of booze bottles overnight. But she does have a choice. She can relieve boredom by accepting a date from a passenger, in which case she still ends up in the cocktail lounge.

She can walk through the Valley of the Dolls to control her weight, or she can pop sedatives in the galley to turn down the emotional attack caused by her work milieu.

In the midst of that totally degrading job, the stewardess, who has been sold on its glamor, its importance, and the special skills it requires, quickly comes to understand management's attitude toward the job and what is really expected.

In a letter to the membership during negotiations, a union officer reported a conversation he had had with the airline's president:

"In conversation with the company president, he asked me where else a group of people with *no marketable skills* could earn so well. I asked him if that meant that we were unskilled labor; he backed down immediately and suggested that our skills were in serving the food."

The fact that so many airline executives have Air Force backgrounds may very well account for the macho attitude toward women employees, reducing them totally to onboard cocktail waitresses, but it bodes ill for an environment encouraging the mental health of employees.

And what of the women who complete college degrees and then are told that in order to be hired they need only supplement that baccalaureate with eight weeks of Katherine Gibbs? Then when they are hired, they can't even use the skills they got at Katherine Gibbs, because they just found out that the real job is to go for coffee, to go for papers, to go for a nice birthday present.

Contrary to the experiences of most women, I can say in my lifetime I have applied for probably 10 to 12 administrative jobs, but I have yet to have anybody ask me how fast I type. Yet it is almost impossible for women to apply for a job without being asked that question. I think that it is obvious that a vulnerable person could easily develop symptoms of mental illness in such an environment.

Dr. Rachelle Warner completed a study of working women in March 1975, questioning those women whose jobs were lost due to the energy crisis. She checked three indices of stress: psychosomatic indices (tension headaches, nervousness, insomnia, dizzyness); depression-withdrawal measures. Responses to questions such as: "Did you feel like not going to work today? Is it worth it? Do you want to?" all came back totally negative toward the job or even getting one's body in motion in the morning; and finally, subjective measures of general health.

What she found is that among employed women those indices are about double what they are for men. But among unemployed or mis-employed women, women whose jobs had been impacted, it ran four times as great—34 percent of the women as opposed to 9 percent of the men. She further reported the difficulty that working women have in getting help and counseling—somebody to talk to. She pointed out, for example, that white-collar women and white-collar men generally have the resources to go to professional help, and blue-collar men lean on fellow employees and on their wives. Blue-collar women have nowhere to go and no one to talk to, least of all their husbands. In almost every case the male reported receiving positive support from his wife and in almost no case did the woman indicate positive support from her husband. So we are going to have to look at those environmental conditions around the job and recognize that those environmental conditions are going to give us the greatest difficulty in terms of mental health on the job.

How about the question of employer responsibility? Is an employer morally responsible for the mental health of his employees? Ten years ago—and it is still true today—Harry Trice of Cornell said in *The Journal of Occupational Medicine:* "The question is moot. Nobody cares what his moral responsibilities are. Workmen's compensation, court actions, and arbitration awards have made clear that the obligations are legal. His thoughts about social responsibility are totally replaced by his fiscal liability."

Workmen's compensation awards and arbitration awards have gone down the path from, early in the game, recognizing the compensability only of the job-related accident, proceeding then to recognizing the compensability of the job-related illness, such as black lung. More recent workmen's compensation awards then decided that accident-related mental illnesses were compensable. That is, one developed a mental illness as a result of physical trauma on the job. The most recent decisions have been to reward the compensability of work-related mental illness, even in the absence of a physical trauma. The acknowledgement that certain jobs and their environments create mental illness has been recognized by compensation boards awarding compensation payments in such cases. Similarly, arbitration awards have consistently led in the direction that discharge, which is the capital punishment of the industrial world, is an inappropriate response to a troubled employee; that the employer has a contractual obligation to support the employee and not to discharge; that the purpose of discipline is correction, not punishment and, therefore, the employer has a legal obligation under a union contract not to discharge the employee but to keep him on and be supportive. So we need not get into the discussion about what his social responsibility is; his fiscal liability is clear.

The next question we have to deal with is, who's qualified to identify and to deal with employee mental health problems? The supervisor? Probably not, he has enough to do and enough different perspectives so that adding the requirement that he identify the emotionally disturbed employee is totally unreasonable. As a matter of fact, Cornell conducts a series of seminars, called "Supervising the Troubled Employee," that deal specifically with the question of what the role of the supervisor is. It surely is not the role of a paraprofessional or professional social worker. Clearly the responsibility is supervising. But something must be done with the troubled employee. How about the company medical staff? I tell you from the point of view of labor that labor won't buy it. Won't buy it because of our experiences in occupational safety and health. We found out that the company doctor doesn't work for us, he works for management. Shockingly enough, in a number of instances in occupational health, the reason given that indications of an employee's poor health—X-rays, medical tests, what-have-you—were given to the employer and kept secret from the worker was becuase of doctor-client confidentiality. Astounding. Now that we have found out that the doctor's "confidential" relationship is to whoever pays him and not to who is the patient; don't ask us in the areas of prevention to disclose to the company's medical staff that we have an emotionally troubled employee. It is absolutely impossible for a worker to trust a company doctor, or a company psychologist, or psychiatrist to any extent that would permit that person to offer treatment.

We think there are two areas, treatment and identification, to which our attention must be directed. We feel strongly within the labor movement that the best mode of identification is peer identification. The person most likely to recognize deviant behavior and to assist one into treatment is the co-worker or the union shop steward who is there on the job—first of all because he notices deviant behavior quickly and, secondly, because he already has the confidence level that enables him to discuss personal problems.

The Long Island Labor Agency for Community Services is currently engaged in a program to train union counselors in community services, alcoholism and drug addiction programs. The counselor is being trained to act as, not the old familiar information and referral agent, because the role of peers and shop stewards is far more than referral, but as an information and assistance agent who stays in touch with the troubled employee while he is in treatment. In terms of that treatment, clearly it must be in a program handled by professionals, separate from the line responsibility of the company.

There are some companies where it works to have a separate staff function within management; there are other companies where it will not and the program must be conducted outside the company entirely, but with a good deal of close communication among the union and the patient and the company.

The last question: What can we do to prevent and to treat job-related mental illnesses? We think we have come close on the treatment aspect. We have learned that the combination of problem identification by peers and of supervisory pressure in terms of work performance can bring people into treatment. Our experience with the alcoholic and with the drug addict is that the family can go down the drain, the community can go down the drain, and a lot of other human relationships can do down the drain, but one must hold on to the job, because the job provides the wherewithall for the purchase of the next bottle of alcohol or the next dosage of drugs. If an employee is to be moved into a treatment program, then the necessary coercion has to do with the threat of the loss of his job. We are saying that a supervisor can take the stance that he has no jurisdiction over what the person's problems are; he deals exclusively with job performance. You're late, you're absent, you're having accidents, you are endangering people around you. The supervisor doesn't make personal judgements. He puts pressure on poor work performance only. It is critical at that point to have union or other worker representatives there, ready to remove the worker into a treatment program when that worker says, "Wait a minute, I don't want to lose my job, I'll take counseling, I'll talk to somebody." We have found over and over that the threat of job loss will motivate the worker to seek help.

In spite of the tendency of companies to develop mechanisms to prevent hiring "problem workers," they are still going to hire a lot of wrong people. We simply have not identified any mechanism for recognizing the employee who will be a potential problem. We are all aware that, in the past few years, more and more companies have become reluctant to hire people because they are "over-qualified." The thinking seems to be that if we hire you, you are going to be unhappy and if you are unhappy, you are going to be a troublemaker, and we don't need any trouble around here. Unions have to be concerned about this whole question of misfits in industry to avoid a general rule that it is important not to misfit people in jobs. If we accept such a rule we are going to find a heck of a lot of people who should be working, not working anymore. If worker and job don't fit, let us consider redesigning the jobs.

That goes to the heart of the question: How do you prevent mental illness? It is the position of unions that the current efforts being made to take a more humanistic approach toward work productivity and work democratization are quite literally the only way we can go to change the work environment to give the worker an opportunity to utilize his skills and his talents.

Teams of workers, we have found in any number of instances, can agree themselves to shift the responsibilities they each have, so as to meet what the peer group recognizes as the talents of each. Such a pattern permits each employee to have a real voice in how the job is designed, and how it works, and what everybody does, what we call work democracy.

We have had enough fragmentation of work by time-study engineers. More flexibility can improve productivity. If productivity is defined as more units per hour, if you mean more kids in a classroom, if you mean more automobiles per day off the assembly lines, then you are denigrating the jobs. What we mean by productivity is not more children per teacher, but a better-educated student. What we mean by productivity is automobiles that aren't lemons. What we mean by productivity is employees with airlines and railroads who leave the customer with a good feeling. That is what we mean by productivity. If you want to improve the worker's productivity, to make his contribution more valuable, then we think the time has come to clearly look at all those areas where we can humanize the workplace. Give the worker a voice in defining and describing and carrying out his own job.

By controlling the environment we may very well be able to knock out the danger of three coincident stress factors. Environment is the only one we can reach and it is the one we are going to attack. The concept of a safe and healthful work place, incorporated in the Occupational Safety and Health Act, must be expanded to include the impact on mental health of the work place.

DISCUSSION

Chaired by speaker Sanford Lenz, the labor panel included:

Anthony Costaldo, AFL-CIO Representative, United Way of Nassau-Suffolk
Calvin Hutchings, M.A., Counselling Psychologist, Air Line Pilots Association
Ed Nelson, Senior Counselor, Local 504, Transport Workers Union
Deputy Inspector Tracy Smith, Nassau County Police Department

Audience:

Would labor consider funding religious institutions to provide the essential psychological support that people need in times of trouble?

Mr. Costaldo:

We work with churches now. Now as far as funding, the union structure is based on dues and there are certain restrictions on what those funds must be used for. You wouldn't be able to get funding from most locals because they are not geared for that. We go to people for funds. We look for money for projects.

Mr. Lenz:

That question hits a nerve. The unions have tried to bring to the attention of funding agencies and service agencies the fact that our people, too, have problems. We have been told for years that those are our problems, we should pay for them ourselves because unions are wealthy. Unions have consistently heard that. Union administration, which is paid for by its dues, does not develop surpluses. The wealth that you hear about in the unions is generally in funds which are employer contributions toward welfare plans. Federal restrictions are so severe in terms of how we invest money and what we are going to put it into, that they preclude unions being a logical source for funding. Unions, however, are a resource for fund raising through their members. Working people have voluntarily contributed $1.6 million to the United Fund, which helps fund counseling within the churches. For instance, Catholic Charities trains their parish priests in community services. So, through our voluntary contributions to the United Fund, we are already paying for religious counseling.

Audience:

I work with school children whose parents are suffering really severe emotional disorders; we see it through their children who are barometers of a great deal of what is going on in the home. Most of these people don't need, and can't afford, hours and hours on a couch. They need support services.

Mr. Lenz:

They need peer assistance, working people helping other working people. Nobody I know is in a better position to check on elderly citizens every day to make sure they are all right, than the man who comes with the mail. A postal worker can be trained to take note of these people and instead of just delivering the mail, he can ring the bell and ask, "How are you today?" Postal workers, barbers, bartenders, and members of other unions can be extremely helpful to people with problems. For instance, we are now training teachers so they can help children who live with alcoholic parents.

Audience:

The Air Line Pilots Association has negotiated a contract with one of the major airlines, which stipulates that if profits drop below 2 percent the pilots will forgo a portion of their salary. This was aimed at keeping pilots employed.

Mr. Hutchings:

As you indicated, it is a means of preserving their employment. We have also seen that happen on a voluntary basis with other companies as a means of protecting the pilot's job.

Mr. Lenz:

There have been a number of instances where plants have shut down for two weeks to avoid a layoff. Instead of laying off 80 people we just shut down and, after two weeks, everyone comes back to work together. There are instances like that, but they do not fit what normally ought to be the pattern. Let me be very frank about why. There is an atmosphere which dictates that union and management are on opposite sides of the table. Union comes in and says, "We would like the right for the worker to participate in the management of the company." The management's answer is, "You go back to work, we are responsibile to the stockholders, you are not. We have the right to manage and the responsibility of managing; no, you may not see our books; no, you may not participate in company decisions." At another time they say, "We would like you to help us by taking a wage cut."

Are we partners, or are we adversaries? We'll play the game either way. But don't tell us that we are adversaries when you are doing well and partners when you are in trouble.

Audience:

If profits fall below 2 percent does anyone in management have to take a wage cut?

Mr. Lenz:

Most managements do not agree that management's salaries are a proper subject for negotiation with the union and, therefore, I can assure you, you will not find them in any contract.

Audience:

I'd like to hear more about training people for community services, peer counseling training.

Mr. Smith:

Our training in the Police Department starts from day one. We go on to a series of inservice and advanced training periods which can run up to two weeks at a time in the Police Academy. Several of our officers have attended special courses in order to become alcoholism counselors. Our training is constant and ongoing. We like to think that it is about the best in the country and we don't hesitate to go to private industry to learn. We develop specialists in all areas of police work whether it is giving a tracheotomy. delivering a baby, or taking a gun away from an emotionally disturbed person; and we are developing inhouse specialists to help our disenchanted employees or our problem employees.

Mr. Costaldo:

We contact the 400 unions in this area to let them know that we are starting a community services counseling course. Union men and women, representing many types of occupations, register for our courses. We recruit our speakers from the many helping agencies that are part of the United Way. Our people learn counseling skills and, at the same time, they learn how to refer people for further help. We also run courses for companies. We involve anybody and everybody who wants to know how to help people with problems. There are many many different types of facilities and services that are available, so one of our prime concerns is to educate people to know about them and use them.

Mr. Lenz:

Our training courses for union counselors consist of two parts, information and assistance. After listening to each speaker, the counselor finds out who to call in an agency for assistance. We train our counselors to listen and to be supportive and to help people solve their own problems. If we feel that a particular agency can be of assistance, then we give people a hand getting to that agency and help them navigate the system. We get about 20 speakers from different agencies. They don't just explain what their own agency does. They explain how the different agencies interact and they give us telephone numbers of the people in the other agencies to call. You'd be amazed what a great booklet of telephone numbers you can develop this way.

Audience:

Is this on a volunteer basis?

Mr. Lenz:

Absolutely. They come in at night for three hours for nine or ten weeks, with two speakers per night.

Audience:

I believe two types of misfits are caused by the union's seniority system, the disenchanged worker who is bumped, and the worker who has moved into a job for which he is not prepared. During a recession, do unions rethink their position on seniority?

Mr. Nelson:

We closed down a Florida overhaul base and our union negotiated with the company to let people who didn't want to move to New York take early retirement.

Mr. Lenz:

The fact that we fall back on seniority does not mean that we don't think about the problem. We know that seniority is a compromise mechanism. Unions are trying to think of better ways, but frequently they will not come up with an alternative and will revert to the seniority system. But that does not mean they haven't given it thought. Any union officer is subject to pressure from a senior member who says, "I want to keep my job full-time, let the young guy go," and also to pressure from the the the low-seniority guy, who says, "Look, let's share this misery somehow." The ultimate decision, very frankly, depends on the makeup of the union, as often as it depends on the rational wisdom of the union leadership.

Mr. Costaldo:

It is up to the individual local and its members how they work it out with management. If seniority is in the contract, you haven't got a right to waive it unless everybody agrees.

Mr. Smith:

Certainly, the worker who is bumped is a disenchanted worker, but I'd like to talk about the disenchanted worker who is on the job. Take, for example, a man who has geared himself up to be a teacher but who finds when he comes out of college that there are no jobs. So he takes a Civil Service exam and becomes a police officer. All of a sudden he finds himself walking a foot post until three o'clock in the morning, saying, "What the hell am I doing here?" So here you have a disenchanted employee and, on top of that, a thousand citizens dependent on that one man's actions. His disenchantment can affect a great many people.

The constant regeneration of interest, so that the man performing a mundane task for seven hours a day is prepared to deliver a baby, or prepared to come to your house when you have suffered a coronary is a very, very difficult task and we are only starting to look at it.

Mr. Lenz:

We are really talking about the mismatched. Management says if the employee doesn't fit the job, change the employee. On the other hand there are some of us who think that maybe management should change the job. Unions have the responsibility to tell management that we will look at the mismatched and see what we can do about them, but management must assume the responsibility for taking a look at the job and the environment in the workplace to see what can be improved. That kind of thing is subject to what we call "nonadversary bargaining" for unions and companies that have moved certain things off the negotiating table. Some excellent alcoholism programs have resulted from this kind of joint effort.

Audience:

I am in vocational rehabilitation counseling and I deal with individuals who are union members who have lost their jobs because of disability of one kind or another. From my own experience of being handicapped, I can see that both union and management are prejudiced or uninformed about disability, and, consequently, in order to maintain a good relationship, they will sacrifice the one individual who is going to give them trouble. I am a union delegate myself so I know that a person with a problem can, at times, become difficult to deal with for the union delegates, as well as for management. So, therefore, you say, well, we have done enough for him, let him go. I would like to find another way to handle this problem.

Mr. Smith:

For one thing, I recognize the fact that a handicapped worker almost always has more to offer in the way of perseverance and fortitude than the average person has. We have a police officer who is a paraplegic answering our telephones. We have a police officer who is partically paralyzed by a stroke, dispatching orders. They are both doing an excellent job and they are not a burden to the police department and they are not a burden to the county because we didn't have to pay to train them.

Mr. Hutchings:

I think there are some things that labor can do in a very constructive manner in dealing with disability. There are medical conditions which should be evaluated and looked at carefully to determine whether, in fact, restrictions are indicated. Is the standard too strict? Is it possible for the person to continue to do his job? Is job termination necessary, or unnecessary? For example, alcoholism is a mandatory disqualifying illness for airline pilots. Historically, any pilot who has ever had a clinical diagnosis or medical history of alcoholism could never again pilot an airplane, even if he had had 15 years of sobriety. He was grounded because of that diagnosis. Now is that realistic or does that situation need to be evaluated?

The association is taking a very active role in looking at this question. In the whole general area of maintaining a continuing ability to work, we are looking at preventive approaches to illnesses and at conditions that may be disabling. We are educating association members to act as information/referral resource persons for health-oriented programs.

Mr. Nelson:

Most unions have negotiated into the contract some sort of long-term disability, so that if a person is totally disabled and can't work, a certain portion of his salary is covered by insurance. Also the Central Trades Council has a rehabilitation center where a worker can be retrained for another job. Unions are very much aware of the handicapped, and we do have agencies and functions to assist them.

Audience:

In the context of humanizing the work place you mentioned the approach of redefining productivity to stress quality output, rather than quantity output. Are you finding management sympathetic to this idea? The bottom line always seems to be dollars and cents.

Mr. Lenz:

Dollars and cents is always the bottom line. No union can sell work humanization or the raising of morale if it can't illustrate that the company is going to make money because of it. We are going to have to demonstrate to companies that it is better for them and their products. Larger companies are willing to experiment the most. The owner of a machine shop with eight employees is not likely to try a test program. Somebody else is going to have to show him what is better and then he may try it later.

At the county level, we are now helping to set up a central committee of government, business, and labor officials to start developing some suggestions in areas of work humanization and productivity. It has got to be at that level if the small guy is ever going to get to take advantage of it. There is just no way you can reasonably expect him to experiment, because if he fails, he goes bankrupt. Trends will have to be developed by the big corporations.

We do see creative and successful experiments going on now in terms of democracy on the job. I am not talking about flash-in-the-pan stuff, where you play nice music for the workers and after three days productivity goes up and then it goes back down. I am talking about programs where a worker is convinced that he has a real investment in his job and that management sees him in the same light.

Audience:

In management by objective programs, management sets the objectives and the employees work towards those objectives as they see fit. I was wondering if unions are attempting to talk about management by workers in the sense that, you along with the management, define what your objective is rather than having management tell you the objective.

Mr. Lenz:

The management by objectives program as conducted by the American Management Association is the way you described it, management and labor meeting the same goals. The answer to your question, and it is true of any question, about what unions do, is yes, some do, and no, some do not. The sharing by management and the worker of the selection of objectives and the planning of strategies is clearly a trend on the upbeat. Whether it is a fad or whether it is going to go on forever, there is no way to tell. Do unions want to do it that way? The answer is yes, if you are in certain unions, no, if you are in others. It varies all over the lot. But there is more and more of this whole idea of democracy on the job. More and more unions are at least listening and trying to work at it and more and more managements are being responsive.

CHAPTER 7

Closing Remarks

SHERMAN N. KIEFFER, M.D.*

To be able to summarize a conference like this is obviously an impossible task. I am fortunate, however, that many of the talks summarized themselves.

Commissioner Bienstock, the first speaker, shared with us a set of 27 statistical tables and charts. He sounded more optimistic, I think, than most of us expected regarding the labor situation in the future. Many of the charts graphically portrayed a variety of employment and unemployment trends. Some were primarily descriptive of our recent and current economic trends and were not directly related to the problems of individuals being over-educated, under-trained, or mis-trained. On the other hand, many of the charts did demonstrate the relationship of such variables as disease, sex, color, socioeconomic status, military status, and other demographic factors to the availability of certain jobs in the job market and to their role in generating so-called employment "misfits."

Most of us were surprised when he pointed out that since 1969, especially in the central cities, there had been a decrease of almost 650,000 jobs in areas

*Sherman N. Kieffer, M.D., is Professor and Vice Chairman, Department of Psychiatry and Behavioral Science, School of Medicine, Health Sciences Center, State University of New York at Stony Brook. Dr. Kieffer earned his M.D. degree from the University of Minnesota and, prior to coming to Stony Brook, was the Associate Director for Patient Care, National Institute of Mental Health. Dr. Kieffer is a consultant at several hospitals, including South Oaks.

where people were not trained or skilled, and related the impact of this on the availability of existing employment spots. For working women, he pointed out the dual job pressures under which they operate, mainly at home and on the job. Most women, he said, really work for economic needs rather than for the needs motivated by the feminist movement. He also pointed out the inverse relationship between socioeconomic status and unemployment. Regarding college graduates, Mr. Bienstock had an interesting table showing the relationship between those who major in social science and humanities and those who graduate in education and business. Some might choose to differ with his thesis about the great advantage of being trained in education these days. I wondered if he was referring to individuals with degrees in business administration or to people with typing or secretarial skills when he used the term "business."

Following Mr. Bienstock we had Dr. Meineker, who is a psychiatric consultant for a top-level insurance company. While acknowledging that psychiatry certainly has a rightful role and is even somewhat at an advantage as a "medical approach" in the management of the kinds of problems with which this conference is concerned, Dr. Meineker made the point that psychiatry per se has some limitations vis-a-vis the more dynamic perspectives of the other behavioral sciences, e.g., psychology and sociology. I am sure that he did this knowing full well that such a pronouncement might raise the hackles, among other things, of his analytically oriented colleagues. He went on to warn that psychiatric intervention carries the additional risk of branding the employee with the traditional stigma still rampant in our society of being "mentally ill."

With this caveat, Dr. Meineker pointed out that psychiatry had two major roles to play in the prevention and treatment of the "misemployed" workers. One was to help identify the employee who might be a high risk for social or emotional disabilities through pre employment screening and by on-the-job monitoring of the employee for evidence of maladaption. The second major role for the psychiatrist was to provide treatment for employees with manifest emotional problems.

The process of pre-employment screening, as helpful as it might be, he saw as a process fraught with dangerous pitfalls. One important pitfall was inherent in his questioning the validity of clinical prognostication. He asked the searching question: Does the identification of an emotional problem or syndrome in an individual really spell failure for a specific job? If not, is such a process fair to the prospective employee? Another seed of doubt about the usefulness of psychiatry was sewn when he noted that disagreement is frequently found between the views of management and those of psychiatrists regarding the ideal personality structure for a particular job. A further common complication in recent years is the strong impact of the equal opportunity requirements on this type of screening.

All factors considered, it was his conclusion that the most important single predictor of job success in pre-employment screening was the degree of "motivation" of the employee. Since he considered this to be even more important than the assessment of "ability," he felt it was an appropriate area for major involvement and consideration by a psychiatrist.

Insofar as monitoring employee adjustment, he felt that the psychiatrist should act in concert with other medical department personnel, first-line supervisors, and middle management by playing a "team member" role in reviewing such symptoms as absenteeism, accidents, and other symptoms of maladaptive behavior.

A particularly cogent point was made in describing the role of the psychiatrist as a consultant to the medical department, primarily because of the unusual frequency with which emotional conflicts at work present themselves first as physical complaints in the medical clinic. With proper early identification of this phenomenon, the employee could be helped to develop better coping mechanisms and could be helped immeasurably by avoiding being over-laboratory tested and over-medicated.

To further delineate and support his position that psychiatry was most useful in the treatment of employees with emotional problems, Dr. Meineker shared with us some representative and illustrative clinical material from his own extensive practice in this area.

Dr. Meineker was followed by Mr. Knowles, the Personnel Director of Grumman Aerospace Corporation, who presented us with an outstanding glossary of definitions useful in gaining an understanding of the term "misfit." He reassured us that eventually all of us are going to fall victim to this dread disease "if we don't watch out." He felt that this is a realistic perspective since some of the surveys to which he alluded showed that 80 percent of the work force population are not happy with what they are doing or would prefer to be doing something else. He then proceeded to trace the natural history of how one becomes a "misfit" by presenting a typology of the psychological, educational, physical, and emotional factors associated with becoming a "misfit." He tied this in with his concept of "coping behavior." After examining the educational system and the problems it faces in preparing individuals for the work force, he concluded that there are three major things wrong with it. One is the curriculum. Another is inadequate career information and orientation. The third is the inept guidance counselor system. The major factors that predispose a person, in his view, to becoming a "misfit" are his personal psychological inadequacies, the educational process, and the influence of government and society.

Granting that industry itself may indeed be profit oriented, he contended that industry recognizes its social responsibility and has adapted a more behavioral approach to its employees and to the quality of their lives. After listing a variety of categories and conditions of "misfits" in industry today, he divided them into two major groups: misfits who were so when they entered the work force, and misfits who became so as a result of employment. With regard to the former, he viewed industry's role as essentially minor. In the area of training the employee once he is engaged, however, he presented an exhaustive list of positive approaches that organizations could take to minimize the production of "misfits." This can be further enhanced, he stated, by career development activities, career counseling activities, good employee relations, maintenance functions, and hygienic functions.

The presentation by Dr. Goldenhar helped to explain the origins and functions of a new medical species—the "primary physician," which he equated with the "family physician."

After taking the conference planners to task for using the term "misfits," which he felt had a pejorative connotation, he described the genesis and evolution of the relatively new medical specialty, Family Medicine, culminating in 1969 with the creation of the American Board of Family Practice which now has a membership of over 10,000 diplomates. He referred to the family physician as a "conduit" into the health care delivery system who deals with the physical, emotional, and social problems of family groups from the "cradle to the grave." He stressed the importance of training in the behavioral sciences for such physicians as an indispensable tool for involvement in preventive as well as therapeutic medicine.

Work, he felt, was a "key to good mental health" by virtue of its importance in the development of a person's self-esteem. It was the dynamics of working, the feeling of a competence associated with mastery and the recognition gained from others for doing something valuable, that he felt was important for most people. Since persons in distress frequently turn first to their family physician, he felt that medicine was obligated to reassure and to allay the anxiety associated with stress by dealing with the person as a whole rather than approaching him in a super-specialized manner based on discrete organ systems.

Chronic dissatisfaction with one's work, he identified as the number one medical problem in industry. He also identified monotony, boredom, lack of reward, lack of satisfaction, and unsuitability as stress producing factors in industry. These may in turn account for such symptoms of behavior as alcoholism, drug abuse, obesity, alienation, and serious family pathology. He regarded unemployment as the ultimate "mis-employment" describing its adverse effects on physical, mental, and social well being manifested by associated increases in suicides, homicides, and crime.

Dr. Goldenhar cogently identified a variety of physical and emotional factors prominent at different stages of life that tended to weaken normal defense mechanisms, thereby reducing a person's capacity to cope with work-associated problems which were easily managed in prior years—middle-life crises, aging problems, authority problems, etc. Since there could be no single panacea for all, he stressed the importance of flexibility and versatility on the part of the physician so that he could employ a variety of therapeutic approaches tailored to suit each individual's needs.

While stressing the point that physical symptoms are frequently manifestations of underlying psychological problems, he made a plea for the beneficial effects of a "thorough work-up." After sharing with us some current findings regarding the relationship among different categories of mental illness and social class and economics, and after presenting some tips on diagnosis and psychotherapy, he concluded his remarks by making a plea for the rightful role of the family physician on the mental health team organized to prevent and to treat mental health problems in our work force.

Professor Neff presented us with a scholarly and historical analysis of the educational process as one of our major academic institutions and of the world of gainful employment as it has evolved in our society. He aptly described one of the underlying concerns of our conference—the mental health problems associated with an individual who might be over-educated but under-trained for the kind of employment that is available in our contemporary society. The implicit, but inevitable, sequelae of this lack of congruence between education, training, and employment are a sense of frustration, dissatisfaction with one's work, thwarted and distorted aspirations, etc. All of these are bound to spill over and present themselves overtly or covertly in the guise of mental health problems.

To determine whether, in fact, there was a developing mental health problem in our society because of this alleged gap between education and employment, he asked some critical questions and wondered whether the results of such exploration might be helpful in developing recommendations for an educational policy as well as for a social policy. He started by taking a close look at the educational enterprise itself in the United States, which he called the classical country of mass public education, and shared with us the definition of the American Association of School Administrators, who in 1966 published a list of nine basic imperatives of our educational system.

He also observed in passing that such a view was a long way from the "Three R's;" that preparation of children for adult work was only one of its many obligations; and lastly, that perhaps we have assigned the schools a set of tasks that may be virtually unachievable, expecting the schools to act as home, family, church, and other social agencies as well. Is it fair then, he asked, to blame the schools alone for generating the problems of the "over-educated?"

Noting the dramatic shift in school population over the past bicentennial period from a tiny minority in 1776 to 99 percent of children between ages 6 and 17 being in school in 1977, he examined the reasons for the enormous expansion of our formal educational system to the point where it seems to have developed a life of its own. For millions the system is one in which the end and the means seem indistinguishable. The great strides of our technology forced the creation of an educational system to keep up with it. One of the basic principles of democracy, equal opportunity for all, forced its expansion through sheer numbers into an educational system which became so enormous and complex that it became a major social institution itself.

Space does not allow for the deserved reiteration of the perceptive observations Dr. Neff shared with us as he continued to explore the relationship between gainful employment, the world of work, and formal education. The same applies to the insightful analogies that he drew between our educational system and the world of work. Many requirements imposed by the world of work are first encountered in the child's world of education such as, separation from family, regularization of habits (clock watching if you will,) accommodation to strangers, punishment and reward systems, conformity vs. non-conformity, meeting of standards, etc. Major differences seem to be that the primary rewards in the school system are in the area of cognitive skills or intellectual achievement. For the bulk of the population, however, there does not appear to be much relationship between school learning and the kind of work one is required to do. Even the extensive vocational school system developed in our country did not provide the answers to some of the critical questions that he raised.

He concluded his discussion by asking the $64,000 question: Can we expect large numbers of cases of lack of fit between a person's education and the kind of work available to him? Assuming a drastic lack of fit, can we anticipate for these people serious psychological problems? Finally, how serious is this problem? His answer was that the problem is more serious in the middle levels of education and work than at the extremes. Those at the upper extremes have more alternatives at their disposal. At the lower extreme, it is a matter of rearranging the production process, (assemblyline work), rather than the discrepancy between education and achievement.

Although there are no guaranteed remedies, he pointed out that many are being discussed very seriously. One remedy would be to undertake major and massive changes in the current educational system structure in the direction of viewing future education as a lifelong rather than a youth-limited enterprise. A second remedy is to dramatically overhaul the process and image of vocational education by increasing its prestige and making it available to people of all ages. A third remedy is to expand and to enhance the field of vocational counseling. A fourth remedy is for American industry to develop training institutions itself instead of leaving it to the educational establishment. The final remedy he proposed was the need for wider recognition that there is, in fact, a problem here, a mental health problem as well as an economic and social problem and that it can use all the help that it can possible get from all.

The last speaker, Mr. Lenz, brought to the conference his rich experience in the fields of labor and industrial relations as both an academician and as a community-oriented labor leader. He reminded us that the labor movement has for many years argued that unemployment and under-employment are "two sides of the same coin" and that published unemployment figures are generally deceptively low.

He quoted heavily from the Brenner Report on the relationship between many forms of social pathology and unemployment. He made the point that if a person has taken a job not commensurate with his skills and training, thereby staying out of the unemployment figures, he still suffers considerably in terms of frustration and anxiety and the symptoms associated with them. He also reminded us of the findings of the Cornell conference held 10 years ago on mental health and industry. The questions raised then, he felt, deserved restatement today. In particular, he wanted to take up the question of who is most qualified to deal with mental health problems of employees. His answer stressed the importance of a multifactorial approach, giving simultaneous consideration to three principal factors which must be considered in any discussion regarding the management of mental health problems associated with industry.

The first and most important of these factors was the environmental context of the job itself. How stress producing was it? The second factor was the employee's innate or acquired capacity for coping with stress. The third factor referred to the precipitating mechanism that triggers the breakdown syndrome. To reduce or minimize the possibility of breakdown one must reduce the magnitude of or eliminate at least one of these three major ingredients. Mr. Lenz's thesis was that since there was little one could do to control the last two factors, emphasis must be given to the first; namely, how one can improve the basic work environment itself.

As an example he used the situation of the airline flight attendants (predominately female.) He used the term "flight attendant" rather than "stewardess" because he wanted to make some significant points regarding the simultaneous impact of sexism as well as other stress-producing factors in industry. He went on to describe the plight in which these women found themselves because of attitudes towards women on the part of management, as well as the sexist role in which society casts the traditional "stewardess."

He supported his thesis with additional examples of problems confronting working women in a variety of occupations and professions. While there is no question that the employer bears primary social and fiscal responsibilities for such problems, was he the ideal agent or person to identify and to manage the employee's problem? He contended that this should come from the employee's peers, a co-worker or shop steward. Anyone associated with management, including the medical department, he felt could not be "completely trusted" since they are paid by management. He described a new program of training union counselors for community service, which he advocated to act as information and assistance agents for employees and to stay in touch with them during treatment by professionals unallied with the company.

The last question with which he concerned himself was the popular issue of prevention. The position of labor is that the answer lies in giving the employee a voice in how the job is designed, how it works, and what everybody does.

He concluded that the process which he labelled "work democratization" is the most effective way to control stress factors in the work environment and to prevent the development of mental health problems in industry.

In the discussion groups that followed the speeches on both days, I was impressed with the spirit that prevailed in each group. There was a certain vibrancy, an air of fulfillment, displayed by many participants who reacted as if they were ventilating pent-up feelings which they finally had had a chance to express at a conference like this. It seemed that this was their first opportunity to meet others who shared their problems and with whom they could discuss matters of common interest. In general, the frankness and the spirit with which information was exchanged was salutary and productive.

Index